Howard being hailed in his FX4.

Dear Sonia,

Enjoy!

Love

Howard

19/4/24

LONDON TAXI FOR HIRE

Cab driving from the 1960s onwards

Howard Goldsmith

Contents

Trade Expressions	1
Introduction	1
Chapter 1 *Doing the Knowledge*	3
Chapter 2 *Today, I am a Butter Boy*	17
Chapter 3 *Vehicles, Laws, and Cab Numbers*	23
Chapter 4 *My Working Habits and The Battle for Punters*	31
Chapter 5 *Conversations*	39
Chapter 6 *More Conversations*	43
Chapter 7 *Private and Public Life*	47
Chapter 8 *Minicabs*	57
Chapter 9 *Travellers and Local Passengers*	65
Chapter 10 *Cabs and Drivers*	73
Chapter 11 *Radio, Traffic Flow and Tips*	85
Chapter 12 *Personal Relations & My Longest Journey*	95
Chapter 13 *Bilkers & Social Relationships*	101
Chapter 14 *Seasonal Work Variations*	115
Chapter 15 *London Traffic*	121
Chapter 16 *Tours, Ceremonies, and Embassies*	129
Chapter 17 *Locals (no, not pubs)*	135
Chapter 18 *London by Night and In The Rain*	141
Chapter 19 *Villiers Street WC2 and Other Ranks*	149

Chapter 20 *Day Work, Lost Property and Moving Jobs*   153

Chapter 21 *Pilot Trip to Israel*   163

Chapter 22 *1970s Living in Haifa*   169

Chapter 23 *Yerushalayim*   177

Chapter 24 *Tiberias*   187

Chapter 25 *The Third String*   195

Acknowledgements   197

Trade Expressions
A few words heard on the cab ranks and shelters

Bill	Cab driving licence
Butter boy	Newly licensed taxi driver
Clock	Taxi meter
Dead miles	Driving empty
Flier	Airport job
Flag fall	Initial fare on the meter
Get off	Leave the rank with a passenger
Green badge	All Metropolitan London Taxis
Kipper season	Period of not much work
Journeyman	Driver paid by the number of jobs recorded on meter
Legal	Fare without a tip
Mush	Owner driver
PCO	Public Carriage Office
On the burst	Venue emptying
On point	First on a cab rank
Putting on	Joining a cab rank
Ranking up	Joining a cab rank
Ramble	Method of learning points in a given area. Group participation.
Roader	Journey outside the 6-mile limit of Charing Cross
Set down	Deposit a passenger at destination
Trap	To find a passenger (at last)
Wangle	Learning to drive a taxi
Yellow badge	Specific suburb(s)

Introduction

I wrote the majority of this book about my experiences driving a Taxicab in London in the 1960s. I was born in London 1933. I lived there until I was evacuated in 1939 to Hove, Sussex at the outbreak of war. My early life as an evacuee was with my aunts and cousins in a three up and two down. Post war my parents, joined us on the South Coast. I studied at Hove County School. I worked for a while as a mechanic for Clarks Bakery Hove and when I started the Knowledge in 1958, the only vehicle I had driven beside an electric bread van was my 1933 MG (PA) convertible.

From the concept of becoming a cabby to getting my bill everything was new to me. To cycle right round Eros (alas no longer possible) in Piccadilly Circus and later when working to sit at the Coventry Street rank facing that statue, at the pulsating heart of the Empire was a thrill never to be forgotten.

While driving I encountered the resident London population, and visitors to London. It was the sheer diversity that made me record events and people. I had had enough regular education sitting in a classroom; even though I did manage to gain the Oxford matriculation, I decided no university for me. The majority of the book is written in the present tense, and it was only in 2022 that I set myself the task of getting those words into print.

Mingled in the text are modern developments since those days and later; comments on what it is like to ride in a taxi as an octogenarian. My experiences changed after I had my left leg amputated and I struggled as a passenger into and out of the modern cabs. Only this week I sat as a rider in a taxi with a sunshine roof and a machine to pay by credit card. How times have changed since my first day at the wheel. I rarely divulge my years cabbing but when I do and we begin to natter with the driver, I discover that many present-day cabbies are unaware of the 'Old Days'.

I have introduced an additional set of my taxi driving experiences. These have a thrill missing from London work and make a contrast. I have added cabbing in Israel – Haifa, and then Jerusalem the Holy City, long considered by many as the centre of the world. Utterly different from my previous experiences in Kensington, Chelsea, and Mayfair where I passed so many hours illuminating the streets with my 'Taxi' or 'For Hire' sign blazing.

There is fun and tragedy recorded here, and my pleasure is to move it from the old typewritten pages to the more up-to-date computer and from there, I trust, into a book for publication.

Chapter 1
Doing the Knowledge

Me on the knowledge…

…at day   *…at night*

I decided to be a cab driver when I was working in our hotel at home in Hove Sussex. I saw a few drivers who came down for their annual holidays and they appeared to be affluent, so I decided to occupy myself in London driving a cab when the South Coast Hotel season was over. Only later did I discover that the London busy season coincides with the South Coast hotel season. It was one job or the other for in the winter both jobs are seasonally slack. To become a driver, I needed the 'Knowledge'. I moved up to London and stayed with my future parents in law. I asked around and found that the London General Cab Co. at the start of Brixton Road ran a strong fleet of Black Cabs. This was *the place* to have your cab washed and serviced. They steered me to the PCO in Lambeth who in turn explained I was obliged to study 'The Knowledge of London'.

Arriving at Lambeth and after being accepted, I was handed a booklet containing 450 standard routes through Central London or "runs", as they are defined in the *Guide to Learning the Knowledge of London*, which is produced by the Public Carriage Office. In all, some 25,000 streets within a six-mile radius of Charing Cross are covered, along with the major arterial routes through the rest of London.

A Knowledge Boy with his bike checking the 'run' to see where to look next. He is also marking up any 'points' seen or to be noted.

The prime factor in becoming a taxi driver is a bicycle. This coupled with strong legs if suitably applied, provide one with a green badge. Initially one applies to the Public Carriage Office at Lambeth with demobilisation certificate (discharge after completing compulsory National Service in the Army), plus a document from one's doctor and optician, plus a guarantee of non-criminal record. Next, I was photographed holding a number and then entered into the files of Scotland Yard. Then I was told to return in 28 days and was issued with the book containing 450 different angles across London. This means 350/450 different starting points with varying finishing points.

Today's (21st century) Knowledge Boys are of a new era and have forgotten or perhaps never even knew how to ride a bike so they mount themselves on scooters and drive round London. They don't notice the hills and bumps, the bollards are passed without recollection, and they have no idea that cycling uphill when you are aged 25 or more makes every couple of yards a challenge, needing another breath.

I remembered my way so well that the first winter after pushing my bicycle pedals for a long tiring year, I was able to work and find my way round London in the thickest and perhaps the last of the 'Peasouper Fogs'. Visibility was one or two yards. Driving in a modern FX4 watching the sights and traffic one becomes less aware of the distances and bends in the roads. The real fogs are gone and are now history and different weather conditions prevail, perhaps floods but in those foggy days few motor vehicles were driven as visibility was so limited. Any vehicle could appear and disappear in the blink of an eye. Phew, a crash has not happened. My nightmare was Hyde Park Corner where every car is changing lanes and directions without a kerbstone being visible.

Knowledge Boys mid-winter at Devereux Court WC2.

The original Knowledge is excellent for it takes into account that a resident in a neighbourhood living there for decades, knows all the cut overs in their own manors. If a driver were to err the passenger will quickly correct him. The depths to which 'the Knowledge' delves include the memorising of the sequence of theatres on Shaftesbury Avenue. Would-be cabbies, known as *Knowledge Boys* or *Knowledge Girls*, traverse routes around London, and can be easily identified by the clipboard fixed to the handlebars of their bicycles (then) and scooters (now) showing details of the streets to be learned that day.

Initial procedures completed, at the PCO clutching my black and white 'Blue Book' I went home and considered the varying advice proffered by other would-be cab men. I decided I would do 5 runs per day. To prepare for this, in the evening I opened a large-scale map on the table. I read the first run printed in the Blue Book and laid a cotton between the two points 4 miles apart, one a tube station and the second an obscure square in the middle of a labyrinth in Islington. This route remains a never to be forgotten string of roads in the mind of anyone who has ever done the Knowledge.

I did not then understand that to a person living thereabouts in the labyrinth that this was home; everyone and anyone who lived there knew all the streets without thinking. Next, I made a note of all the streets which ran most parallel to the cotton, jotting down the left or right turns needed to keep moving forwards. Then, I chose a random route from the 450 which started somewhere near the end of the first. It ran from the Northern Polytechnic now the University of North London, to an hotel. Then from a police station to a hospital, theatre to dogs' home etc. By now I had prepared 5 runs with 10 different starting and finishing points probably 50 different roads, with their related positioning, plus any one-way streets I might have encountered.

Initially, before we were married in January 1959, I lodged with my Mother-in-Law to be, in Essex, now Redbridge. Fixated on getting the cotton line firmly in place I inserted drawing pins through the map and into the dining table so I could tie the cotton in place. Joining the two points together by their 'shortest' cotton route. The only trouble was I had ruined the best and only good table in the house making drawing pin holes in the highly polished surface that the family had preserved for years. By the time I had completed my 5 runs over several days there were nearly 100 pin marks in the highly polished surface. My name quickly became mud.

Early next morning though the weather forecast was for rain, I found my way to the first of the points. This in itself was a 6-mile journey with about 50 'points' en route all of which I sublimely ignored through my ignorance, that nothing is unimportant. That first day was a walkover I noticed very little, cycled as fast as my lungs would permit and decided to do 10 runs the next day and finish the course in half the usual time taken to acquire one's Bill.

On returning home, I 'Called Over' the runs I had just completed including the on the ground corrections which were not clear from the map. One Ways, no right or left turns, no entries. Three months into the Knowledge when we were married my next job was to prepare a meal for my wife who was out earning the wages as a paint and tracer for a West End Advertising Company. Her income tied in with the money my parents were supplying would see us through the year, for there is no remuneration for anyone who takes on the Knowledge. A 'Knowledge Boy' is on his own.

As I prepared my routes for the second day it slowly became clear to me that calling over routes learned would have to be checked by someone listening, otherwise I could be repeating errors. Ah! My wife. Unfortunately, my recitations tended to send her to sleep more often than not. She had been at work all day. By the end of a couple of weeks, months, the number of runs began to multiply and it became impossible to call over every run every day. I continued to put in an 'Appearance' at the PCO The number of runs I had intended to complete diminished because of inclement weather, mechanical bicycle problems, doing the shopping, visiting the launderette, and even though I had not perfectly memorised those runs, rumour had it, and we Knowledge Boys thrived and existed on rumours, that every 'appearance counted as a "mark". I was not unduly put off by the 'come back in 28 days'.

It became necessary to join with other candidates to 'Call Over the Runs' and sometimes debate alternative routes. Three or four would be cabbies, was enough to listen to a run and perhaps mention Points en route. While we chattered, I heard of Knowledge Boys who work through the day and then go out on their bikes at night, in order to have an income during the long study period. I was lucky.

It was said that if one appears keen, arriving at the PCO two or three hours before admittance into the tiny room at the foot of the stairs the examiners who are all referred to as 'Sir' will treat you kindly. Another rumour has it that because there are only a limited number of "Reductions" per day (i.e., from 28 to 21 days; 21 to 14 days) and a limited quota of Bills, a late comer no matter how many questions he or she answers at the oral examination will leave the session disappointed.

A reduction is permission to appear more frequently and is tantamount to passing a preliminary examination. The words "Come back in 21 days" means you have answered sufficiently well and that they would like to see you more often. "Come back in 14 days" means that you are sufficiently advanced to be considered nearly there. So, some Knowledge boys arrive early to avoid the oppressive atmosphere of the little room plus the contagion of the fear which haunts every corner.

For my first Carriage Office appointment I arrived well within the given half hour and was warned that should I have arrived any later I would have been told to come back tomorrow. Everyone was wearing their best suit and everyone had their hair well-greased and combed. What with the wait before the examiners started their questions, plus the wait while they had their tea, it was a full 3 hours before I saw anyone, the last of the 50 candidates to enter the chamber.

When my name was called, I climbed the dreaded stairs and full of trepidation went into the wrong room. A glare pushed me out, and there was I standing at ease as instructed in front of a desk with a seated character shuffling some papers and he asked me to take him from a place I had never heard of to a place I did not know. I managed a bold "No Sir" and only had 4 more questions to answer.

One question that I did answer, by suggesting that I literally drove through Kings Cross Station without stopping, was hilarious. I also was unaware that every question had to be answered with "Set down on the left or on the right", in order that the passenger could safely exit the cab. Running over that appearance in my head that evening I realised I was supposed to be frightened. So, for my future appearances I used a stammer for the only time in my life. At appearance number two I received of course 28 days, but I had remarkably answered one run and if my memory does not err, *two points*.

Conversing during *call overs,* those of us who had not received a reduction, speculated, that perhaps the more moronic the Knowledge Boy the greater his chances of success. Starting with a blank mind and concentrated solely on street names and locations, ignoring Inigo Jones Churches, Adam Terraces, and Nash Crescents there was less information to be absorbed. My next two appearances were fiascos, for I answered not a question. Another story circulating at that time was that

training for the Knowledge can measurably alter the hippocampus of trainee cab drivers. The hippocampus is the area of the brain used for spatial memory and navigation, and is often larger in taxi drivers than in the general population.

A Saturday Ramble.

Everywhere including cul-de-sacs are explored visited and noted. Please note me peeking out from the cul-de-sac. This photo was taken long after my Knowledge studies and there is nary an old-fashioned bicycle to be seen. Photo taken in the good old days when Aldwych was a one-way street.

Somewhere in London in those days (1960s) there appeared to me to be a secret headquarters. The place where the scheme is mounted. It would of course have to be large with many secluded corners. At the end of each day, little men with rosy cheeks would come back stealthily and happily to their secret rendezvous. Their features could be European, and they talked with a certain accent which is not totally English, though they might well be Bretons. They drop their 'Aitches' and sometimes I feel that it is wonderful that they succeed in understanding one another.

Should a stranger walk among them he might well walk with care for when they exhale even the strongest Londoner must flinch. They are trained from early in life to ignore this odour and are immune to it – in fact it is part of the plan. Suddenly one night in the middle of the imaginary cavernous hall there would be a lull in the incomprehensible mutterings and then a jubilant cry 'St. John's Wood!!'. The innocent citizens of this neighbourhood probably grunt in their respectable beds, shiver slightly and continue to dream. Little do they realise what a curious scheme is being mounted. For hidden in this building are vehicles which look like old-fashioned bicycles but are specially designed with strengthened carriers able to carry great weights, and occasionally passengers. Plain wooden boards are mounted to protect the strings of alien goods which will descend on the innocents.

On the morrow while the husbands of the of the sober families are away at work in the City or are in the Law Courts earning honest money, the attack starts. Knock, knock at the door. "Bonjour, would you like to ………." Slam, the door shuts violently, and this attack is quickly repulsed. But is repeated elsewhere and slowly and insidiously strings of French Onions enter the homes of healthy Londoners. It is frequently the young housewife mesmerised by a smell she associates with happy events on the continent that is gullible. Perhaps the odour of Gaulloise cigarette smoke plus a touch of garlic, both reminders of happy hours abroad that are enough to let the onions enter yet another London Kitchen and hang from the spare hook on the door. There must be nights when the moon is in the correct phase that the murmuring in the Secret Place is more fervent than usual. It is followed by a longer than usual hush and then a wild yell. A king-sized venture has been planned on the morrow. GARLIC. Garlic is not just on the menu it is on the bikes. Perhaps after their annual ventures some of these men will try their hand at the Knowledge. Either way, they were to fade into history.

At my 4th appearance I was sufficiently petrified to forget where Buckingham Gate is located. Obviously next to Buckingham Palace. Between my 5th and 6th appearances to reassert my ego which had by now reached a nadir I worked outside London assisting my parents in our guest house in Hove, and so had no time for exam-nerves.

On the 6th appearance 5 out of the 6 questions crossed Chelsea Bridge and unknown to the examining officer we were now living in Battersea and used this bridge with its environs daily. Fluent in the surrounding neighbourhoods I received my first reduction. This meant I would have to intensify my studies for I was to appear more frequently. My bike was falling to pieces, and I had already received a warning from the police for driving my vehicle contrary to the prescribed manner i.e., cycling the wrong way in a one-way street!

About this time, I must have completed some 350 runs and I discovered I could join the remaining runs together using the already learned routes. Now I started to learn points. These included buildings which were demolished (Local landmarks) and others not yet completed. I embarked on City (of London) and West End Rambles, every Saturday from 10:00 to 02:00 a hundred or so boys would leave a rendezvous in Aldgate and in groups of about a dozen follow one of the nearly graduated trainees along a set sequence of streets naming each house and club and important restaurant as we went.

There were regular groups of '14 day boys' who waited outside the PCO and asked each trainee as he exited "What came out today?"   In this manner those present and their cronies were aware of the newest

11

points asked. They and the old favourites could be memorised in time for the next appearance.

There is a pleasant fable which every Knowledge Boy dreams will come true, and that is one morning as he awakes, he will have the map of London emblazoned in his memory. Perhaps I had an advantage coming to London from the coast because I started the task with no previous memory of any streets, I had no preconceived ideas such as that the 137 bus took the shortest route between Camden and Streatham. Soon after I began my 21-day appearances I received my reduction to 14 days and on my last appearance answered 20 runs as per 'Blue Book'. Now, I was eligible for the suburbs of London for I like all the Knowledge Boys initially study within a six-mile radius of Charing Cross.

There are suburban neighbourhoods and even Inner London neighbourhoods where my memory fails me for the rare once or twice a year I am called there. I have to ask the rider the best way. He can help because he is aware of the current (time of day) road conditions and is aware of local road works. It is not dissimilar to the architect who has studied cantilever roofs yet never designed one or an accountant who studied company law yet never needed it for the daily grind.

The original Knowledge is excellent for it takes into account that a resident in a neighbourhood living there for decades knows all the cut overs in his own manor and will feel that the driver is taking him for a ride if he takes a longer than necessary way round.

I must admit I learned my suburban routes by rote. I passed my taxi driving test first time, after wangling 'learning to drive a taxi' for two weeks. I felt obliged to work for the firm which had given me a taxi to learn to drive. They had the best 6 months of my work for never again can I emulate the energy and enthusiasm that I had at that time. The Knowledge of London which I needed to become a taxi driver took me 11 months and two weeks to acquire, which was quick. It also took me about the same period of time to learn once I was a cab driver, that the public is tough rude and superior. I quickly had to hide any manners I previously possessed and acquire a veneer of briskness and abuse.

I had received no training in psychology, but I had to deal with that abrupt and contrary group 'The General Public'. This is a group to which no one admits belonging and yet everyone criticises. I learned quickly that a business-like veneer was a necessity. Unless I was tough people thought I was simple and could be exploited. I found myself frequently called upon to aid passengers in their plights. I sometimes felt I was running a mobile Social Service. I evaluated each incident as it cropped up to see if it was genuine and reacted accordingly. I was in a good position to help and felt the obligation that my aid somehow balanced the generosity of more affluent passengers.

The three past years of taxi driving in London (1962), having been buffeted by the public have changed my working persona. Starting somewhat naively, and quite gullible; a provincial and polite youth, I have developed into the accepted image of a hardened London cabbie in order to protect myself against people. Passengers, fellow motorists, and pedestrians.

Saturday nights I almost enjoy driving through Leicester Square as it was then in the 1960s, with through traffic from Coventry Street Corner House to the Hippodrome, making pedestrians jump, for I have slowly become impatient with persons that walk in the road to show off to girls or mates. I have also perfected a malicious glare and can now also create a full smile for the parsimonious passenger.

Driving a taxi is not a simple matter of bluffing a bus driver that you are going to put your small black vehicle in front of his large red one, it is more complicated. A Rolls Royce driver told me he sometimes dares other drivers to scratch his car as he parades through London.

Disability Matters

At the age of 74 some 15 years ago, I had a transfemoral leg amputation. Leaving me 'without a leg to stand on'. Then, as a young 30-year-old, I became aware of maintaining a social conscience something often appreciated by the public but not understood to be part of the job. A by-product of seeing and meeting all sections of the community are thoughtful manners suitable for older people, while maintaining an adding machine in my mind capable of balancing that good last tip with the human responsibility of assisting the elderly. Several times a day the very old and the infirm use my taxi. Their remarks made me ponder on my youth, and healthy strong muscles.

I always wonder when my bones will begin to ache, and sinews refuse to work. "Oh dear, this step is so high" "You don't mind helping me, do you?". My large hand pushes gently in the middle of a small bent back "I broke my leg a couple of years ago and it has never been the same".

At the end of the journey – "You drivers are bricks, the one who took us down to the club was a fine fellow…....it is our only outing all week……..a cab is the only way we can get there….can't walk you see…….it is terrible when you get old….I would not be sorry if I die tonight….. Ada!, he's treated us to the ride!".

However, the step up into the cab or down to the road remains 12inches. Young people do not notice it is there, old people cannot stretch their limbs that far. During the 21stcentury taxi has grown a step which slides out on command, halving the distance between the cab floor and the road. Nowadays (aged 89) in order to exit the passenger compartment, I sometimes sit on the cab floor, thankful that it is washed nightly and proceed from there. This is my safest method of getting my false leg onto the pavement.

A special way to exit.

We regularly drive punters to and from hospitals. "Oh, it is so good to be home again" smiles an old lady as she clambers out of the passenger compartment after a stay in Hospital. She is helped by her husband down the garden path. I remain parked there till the front door key is turned and only then relinquish responsibility for my passengers.

My own fingers cry out in sympathy as I watch passengers whose hands seem to have lost their flesh. An eternity of years must have warped the straight lines of yesteryear, tied them in knots as they try to extract a single coin from a purse. I watch sometimes silently, sometimes jovially. When asked, I aid them, and having driven away wonder fearfully Why? Why? Why?

Like every cab driver, I thought I had a good knowledge of the London streets until one day I drove a man who could not see. He told me the alternative routes I could take if there was unexpected traffic jam. It quickly became clear to me that this man held more in his head than I, and I would get hopelessly lost if I tried to attempt some of the alternative routes he suggested and which he had memorised from his seeing days. I remained fervently on the main roads and we did not have any congestion in front us all the way. My head began to whirl. Would he suggest this route or that route? We were driving through the rush hour and there were four potential jams on the way. As we approached each one, he enquired as to whether the traffic was flowing and was ready with an alternative. He recited the routes as well as any new cab driver and was much more confident. We spoke of many things on that journey, his lack of sight had not deterred him from work and hobbies.

I usually accommodate the passengers who explain at the start that they only have a certain sum of money to spend, or only have a specific sum of money on them, but I do not feel so obliging if this happens at the end of the journey. It is then, I begin to blow my stack.

"I have only got 7/6d will you take me as far as you can towards Putney?". Without demur, I agreed and in fact took the young man as far as he needed. I had decided that the well-dressed young man was genuine and was well aware that there was no alternative transport as midnight was long gone.

"How much will you charge me to Finchley Road Tube Station?" asked a portly individual.
"It goes around 7shillings", I replied.
"Take five" he said knowingly.

"No, what's on the clock!".
"Six" he said hesitantly.
"NO, what's on the clock" I said, and engaged gear ready to drive off.
"Do you know the way? All right take me there for what is on the clock".

By this time, I was furious, if the man's clothes were any criteria, he was wealthy by any standard, and he was just mean. I am convinced that this was just a try on, and I became unwilling to talk with the man.

There are times I get a laugh, when asked for a road the passenger does not want me to realise that he has never visited. He is unaware he has arrived until halfway down the street, I turn round and ask for a house number which we sometimes have passed.

Occasionally, I am paid in dollars. All too often three half-crowns are really two, with a now old-fashioned penny, slipped in between. It is no longer a surprise to be told my tip is thruppence not sixpence, because the clock went up while I was stopping. Compensation for these aggravations resides in the esprit de corps when one cab yields to another on the congested roads. This kaleidoscope of daily contingencies, evens out; the occasional meanness, with the gladness of fraternity of cab drivers one for the other.

Chapter 2
Today, I am a Butter Boy

The moment I became aware that I was qualified and had just passed my taxi driving test I returned the cab to Levy's, York Way N1.and went into their canteen. I sat there and drank a cup of tea to steady myself. The company had lent me a cab to wangle and to do my test. Now was the time to return the favour.

Finally convinced I was ready for the big moment. I telephoned my wife saying I would be back *after work.* That same rush hour I went out onto the road. I jumped into the cab the clerk had allotted me, after I checked that the tank was full of diesel and that the windscreen was clean, left the garage, and drove down the 'Cally' (Caledonian Road) before I realised the 'For Hire' sign was not illuminated. I pulled into the curb and searched around the cab scrupulously, scarcely daring to push and pull all the buttons and levers but could not discover how to light the 'For Hire' sign. Ignominiously I returned to the garage and asked one of the cab washers where the switch for the lights was.

The washers who were usually tipped on arrival back at the garage had the job of washing not just the exterior of the cab but also the floor of the passenger compartment. Of course, taking care that the windows were shiny. Each taxi garage had a staff of night time washers for this was the main time the cabs were all returned to the garage.

The Bill which is displayed is from later in my career. But look at the fee!

I was once more ready to start work and now I was not sure of the best way to begin for I did not want to sit on a rank, so I drove along paying great attention to the traffic probably concentrating to such an extent that I must've missed a few fares.

It was evening during the rush hour, the aura of apprehension and excitement carried me down the Euston Road towards the West End. I wondered how it was possible to see pedestrians waving their arms and hands while I was giving all my attention to the rush hour traffic. But gradually I became aware that the traffic could look after itself and I would look out for outstretched hands. After a couple of weeks, I could not only scan the street for arm movements, on the nearside pavement but also on the far side too. Months later my expertise was such that if someone decided to scratch his face, I was able to differentiate it from a deliberate hailing signal. The best sign of all was when someone stood motionless on the sidewalk, then I quickly took my boot off the accelerator and moved it above the brake pedal identifying the client before he hailed me.

The first person to hail me was a man. He asked me for Waterloo Station ('The Loo') and I was chuffed as I certainly knew where that was and the shortest route. As we drew close to the station, I experienced an ethical problem which I did not know how to solve. There is a half mile circuit to get to the set down point and this entailed going right past the pedestrian entrance to the station. I waited for a shout – none came, and I continued. The punter was inured to the route and made no comment, but I knew that it might well have been quicker and definitely much cheaper to walk the last distance inside the station.

Had I been more experienced I would have set down where I could easily rank up and be in position to have another fare. Later, I knew where to set down to trap someone who was walking to the rank, but that is another story. I now know that when driving to 'The 'Loo'' I might be asked for the 'Side door' or put more simply 'Platform 1', its other name is 'Stage Door'. Sometimes I am asked for 'Underneath the Arches' or the 'Lion' a decoration by the main pedestrian entrance.

'The Vic' should not be confused with the 'Old Vic' or even the 'Young Vic' theatre. The Vic is simply Victoria Station, otherwise designated for set down as 'The Shakespeare' in order to avoid the half mile diversion similar to that at Waterloo Station.

'The Brighton Side or the News Theatre' sets the fare down at the needed side of the station. Phew. I did not realise I knew all that info. and that's only one station.

Today the Brighton Side can be called the Gatwick side. Writing this I am reminded of the man who was '*THE WAVER ON*'. He waved every taxi on the rank in Wilton Road SW1 into Terminus Place. What he was doing might seem a boring job. His job was beckoning onward, taxi after taxi, one after the other. The job however was vastly lucrative, for no one passed him by without paying a 1d, a penny or more. Maybe the *WAVER ON* retired to the South of France! maybe not.

The point of this exercise was that the feeder rank inside the station was not visible from the Wilton Road rank. Any taxi adding itself to this feeder rank, could be *putting on foul,* which would cause bedlam, as there are buses and taxis arriving and leaving and every inch of parking is designated. The area contains the terminus for many bus routes. The underground station access is there too. It is usually a good rank with trains arriving from the South coast, Sussex and Kent, not forgetting Gatwick Airport in later years.

While working, I had to learn the various feeder ranks that supply the major rail termini, and found out during the dead hours and seasons, that sometimes the feeds were really full and the number of cabs waiting made the line extensive. I only learned what was going on, and where to wait by observing the other drivers. The longest waits on feeder ranks were during the 'kipper season'. The slack time of year with little work and drivers had to make do with the cheapest food – kippers.

Having done my first job, I recrossed Waterloo bridge and trapped for Chelsea. I suddenly felt elated I was being paid *and tipped* for driving. I could not believe my luck. What an easy way to become rich. I cannot remember the sequence of jobs after this, except that this was the first time, I returned home for a mid-evening break and meal.

The first night I was out, I was a genuine 'butter boy'. I was asked to drive to Hyde Park Place W2, my fare let me pass his home three times before remonstrating with me for not knowing where he lived. The address which is a part of the Bayswater Road is well obscured, especially if one is concentrating on the fast through traffic which was quickly overtaking my slow-moving cab. He was taken aback to hear a courteous answer and even more offended to be driven by a driver who could use the Queen's *English* as well as himself.

Now on his mettle, he decided that I was rude and abusive, which fact I patiently denied. This type of man was one of the class, who know they are superior and all employees exist to kowtow.
The word "*Taxi*" only came into usage because of the "taximeter" – which calculates your fare. Meters were attached to the "motor cab" in 1907 and that is how the word *Taxi* evolved. The word '*Cab'* goes further back to horse drawn vehicles. "Cabriolet" was a light horse drawn carriage with a folding hood. From the beginning of the

motorised taxi, there had to be a partition separating driver and passengers, which happily prevents drunks from grabbing the steering wheel, and simultaneously provided privacy for the riders. Then Austin and Morris produced the grandfathers of today's cabs. Not so different, but not the same. After WWII, in the early 50s the FX3 model appeared and then it merged into the FX4 during the 1960s. Ergo, this book is about the transition period in the 1960s, years later the cabs became TX4 then TX5.

1954, sitting in my self-propelled 25-pounder Sherman tank, on the Lunenburg Heath in Germany after the second world war doing my National Service, I was blissfully unaware that in the Houses of Parliament they were discussing the future of the London cab trade yet again. I had no idea while in uniform that I would end up driving and later owning a taxi. In the 4th regiment Royal Horse Artillery. I served as a Technical Assistant supplying precise direction, range, cross winds, air temperature, to the guns. 'Officers' had horses. We were allowed to ride them occasionally, but they were no longer used to move artillery weapons in use by the British Army of the Rhine.

Technical Assistant 4th Regiment Royal Horse Artillery 1953

Westminster during this period was considering the Runciman Report on the London Taxi situation. Britain not only had troops in Germany against a Russian threat but was rebuilding itself after WWII and converting the war industry back into a civilian one. The ruins of the bombed houses were being rebuilt as part of the recovery and London was at the heart of it.

Members of parliament were becoming aware that modernisation was key to a stronger economy. The 1953 Runciman Committee found that there was a decline in the number of taxis on the road. A radical approach was called for and one way to aid the taxi service was to exempt taxi buyers from paying purchase tax. In addition, Hire Purchase restrictions from 1952 would be lifted from cabs. Two vital clauses to boost the trade. The November 9 1960 Taxi Debate in Parliament expresses the first indications of a potential duplicate system of taxis which would ultimately manifest itself as *minicabs. Indeed, the word rickshaw was mentioned,* and it took less than a decade before central tourist London was pestered with both.

Chapter 3
Vehicles, Laws, and Cab Numbers

At that time there were many drivers over 70 years of age, a portent of a further decline in the number of cabs on the road. 1953 saw less than 5,500 cabs available in London and under 10,000 licensed drivers, one does not have to be a mathematician or a driver to realise they are not all on the road at the same time. Owner drivers 'Mushes' were just 40%. Later in the 1960s the number had risen to around 6,000 cabs on the road. Today in 2023 there are 21,000 Hackney Carriages licensed by the Public Carriage Office. Perhaps a London symbol, but unrecognisable to me as an ex-taxi driver who knew cabs when a starting handle was essential in case of battery problems. I remember drivers conversing while queuing on a rank and one definitely said "I won't buy a new cab until they find something more substantial than a tiny ignition key to crank it!"

In 1953 journeymen took some 37% of the clock fare, plus extras and tips. Owners at the time, said this worked against them as I will mention later, for the owners complained a driver stopped work as soon as he had earned enough. The owners' expenses not least petrol, diesel, and vehicle parts rose continuously. Diesel cabs became more common later. In the 1960 House of Commons debate it was not understood that no taxi wants to be booked at fixed time and place, for there is no knowing where a cab will be at a given moment. Today in 2023 there is a system in place where a radio taxi can be pre booked, for the dispatcher knows where the working taxis are placed at any time and can arrange for a nearby taxi to pick up a pre-booked ride. I personally have benefited from this system.

The first cab that I drove was an FX3 model taxi which followed on from previous London taxi designs, it had the traditional 3-door body, with an open luggage platform rather than a front passenger seat beside the driver. The FX3 like all London taxis, has a tight turning circle of 25ft (7.6m) diameter, as required by the Conditions of Fitness. It was a Diesel with a manual-gear box. There were heating plugs to give the injectors the hot start that was needed. They were applied for 30 secs though to be sure they did their work I always gave a full minute. The sad alternative was to crank the drive shaft in the engine block. The FX3, was produced for the trade by Austin in 1948, although it was not the first post-war taxicab introduced in England, it was the first modern all steel taxicab. The all steel bodied FX3 was revolutionary and was the standard Black Cab of London. The three-door body design with its open luggage bay continued a pre-war design for taxicabs, but unlike pre-war taxis, the FX3 had a sliding glass partition between the driver's compartment and the luggage bay. Previously, following an earlier fashion the front window, the windscreen, opened to let the wind flow through. Complying with Carriage Office standards of fitness regulations, the roof was built for a gentleman to be seated wearing his top hat. There was room for 4 passengers two of whom could sit on either jump seat.

Everyone should feel safe in a taxi. The story goes that the chassis is strong enough to withstand 2 London Double Decker buses trying to squash it from front and behind?!

Over the years, meddlers and modernisers have tried to tinker with these arcane rules, but they remain in place because they work. The cacophony from the engine was recently nearly sound proofed and microphones make passenger driver conversations possible. [I have added this 60 years later].

Tariff changes are a brief interlude during which tourists and indeed Londoners are bewildered. Every so often, infrequently, an amended tariff is stuck onto the glass partition to be consulted because of fare rises. Today it does not take long for electronic changes to be made to the meter the only delay is getting 16,000 cabs to the meter centre. Once I found a soul mate who watching me calculate the extras and the tariff during a new rise spontaneously exclaimed "Gee, you have trouble adding it together too!" an amicable ending to a journey is like balm on the driver's tedium.

"Mum, why are you laughing at me?" asked the ten-year old lad. The response was immediate in a strong Brooklyn accent. "You should be so good with your school arithmetic as you are with the British money". The boy, maybe a prodigy, had correctly read the fare on the taximeter, converted it to the new tariff stuck on the partition window, added the extras (more than one passenger), and included a shilling tip. All this in the time it took me to apply the handbrake and press the stop button on the meter. The Printed Fare Change stuck to the partition window e.g., 7/9 became 10/- Ten bob. One could say 50p in today's money. I wish I had possessed that lad's agility of mind.

Howard with the new tariff glued to the party window. If the meter records 7/9d the fare is 10/-. The new sticker will be taken down when the meter is updated to the new tariff. Each cab in turn will have its' meter reset. This is an early FX4 window. Later, a special money receptacle was added in the centre.

Perhaps it was the threat of minicabs that made me realise how good my job was. As my employer Mr. Pearce of Battersea Park Road the owner of 26 cabs said to me "It is a Cab Drivers' world". It certainly seemed to be so. As long as I paid 60% of the meter to him and went out to work regularly, there is no other control that he has over me. Usually cabs are worked either by 'Day' men or 'Night' men, the changeover hour being around 17:00. Each driver working about an 8-hour shift. Sometimes if the driver works diligently and does not do too many household shopping chores, and does not spend too much time sleeping, or sitting on remote taxi ranks (where no one can find him) his employer lets him keep the cab all week.

It is a comment on the 21st century, when, well into my first year of driving - 1959, my wife was still turning my shirt collars and cuffs. In those days it was common practice to remove these items from the shirts and reverse them, so that the frayed edges were no longer visible and were worn next to the body. There cannot be too many Londoners who still do this. But it is most unlikely that it would be a cab driver. Today one presses computer buttons, and hey presto chooses any one of hundreds of shirts of varied patterns, colours, designs and prices.

Can you the reader, remember when the choice was telephone OR computer? There was obviously only one telephone line into the house. Who had even heard of broadband?

Laws and fashions change with the years, now we may use the word 'Taxi' illuminated on the front roof, as opposed to the old fashioned 'For Hire'. What a relief it was to suddenly have the use of a central mirror. A driving mirror looking out through the rear window is obligatory in private cars and in as many vehicles as possible. To ensure the privacy of the punters it was missing in London taxis, for many decades. I acknowledge that the wing mirrors show most of the traffic behind the cab but ..., a sudden stop at a zebra crossing could result in rear end collision. Lord forbid, we should look at the riders in the back seat. Previously we could only look in the side mirrors to see who was behind and who wanted to overtake.

Drivers paying a queen's ransom to buy cabs (today it is multiplied many times into an emperor's ransom) were finally able to buy a taxi where the rattling from the engine was sound proofed and they no longer had to shout to speak to the passenger. I suspect in those days, visitors from abroad thought that we were churlish as we did not converse with them. It was simply that it was so difficult to hear what was said. The complication was the glass screen which gives both privacy to the passenger and protection to the driver. We were wallowing in tradition.

Although the FX3 was offered only as a petrol model until 1954, when the diesel variant was introduced, it quickly became the cab of choice especially for fleet owners because of its lower cost of operation. Standards of fitness regulation requiring a 25-foot turning radius were fastidiously maintained. The FX3 continued virtually unchanged throughout the production run, starting post-war and ending in 1958 with the introduction of the FX4. A truly unique piece of London history is embodied in the distinctive shape of the London taxicab of the 1950s.

A reason that the FX4 is not popular with (1960s) owner drivers, is the legitimate complaint that repairs including replacement parts are double the price of the FX3. The automatic transmission costs a small fortune to fix. Fleet owners have the identical gripe. The responsibility of repairs and maintenance dissuaded me from becoming an owner driver for many years. While journeying I merely have to leave a note for the mechanic and the vehicle is repaired and waiting for me the next day, and I don't have to think about it.

Another major expenditure of the mush, are the 'Stop Notes'. These occur when inspectors from the Public Carriage Office descend on the home of the cab owner. Their significance is the greater for there is no previous warning. There was in those days a half rule that vehicles had to be housed in a garage when not in use. This was usually ignored.

A 'Stop Note' would demand repairs be completed before the vehicle is used to carry passengers. This happened to me once when one of my kind neighbours reported the cab for emitting too much black smoke via the exhaust. This same neighbour had previously in discussion with me enquired if there were less fumes on the ground floor where I lived or the third floor where she dwelt. As we both lived in the shadow of the Battersea Power Station I forbore to reply. Those were the days before 'environmental' problems became a major topic and were mainly ignored. Our power station's chimneys excelled in producing prime grime black smoke 24 hours per day.

While *journeying,* 20 minutes was the total time I left the cab on its own and drank a cup of tea and munched a cheese and pickle sandwich, but it was sufficient to have the following defects noted. The report was received by my employer several days later: 1) Brakes out of alignment. 2) Passenger door locks loose. 3) Strap retaining the passenger door loose. 4) Passenger seat springs flat. 5) Window seals worn out. 6) Boot did not close 100%. 7) Minuscule dent in rear wing. 8) Worn Tyre. 9) Sulphur on battery terminal. 10) Oil-leak from Engine. This list was compiled in two shakes of a lamb's tail, with no signs of a visit when I returned to work.

There are other occasions when there is a 04:00 visit by an inspector to a fleet garage. Usually, the result is about half a dozen out of fifty cabs receive a stop. If a cab is not in not there, the absent vehicles are requested to turn up at the PCO for a check of potential defects. The superficial inspection that would have taken place at the garage becomes a major investigation once the cab enters *The Yard*. So, if a cab is called up it has to be perfect. All this is apart from the annual inspection when the vehicle is checked right down to the chassis and everything renewed from there onwards. Additionally, each time the cab changes hands the same procedure must take place. Such is the futility of these tests that an ex-employer of mine bought a cab and after I had driven it for only three days the prop-shaft fell off. So much time is wasted on pedantic nonsense that no attention is paid to vital links.

At that time the dividing glass screen providing privacy for the punter was in two parts, Should I wish to talk I could open the screen which also protects me. But only enough to make a shouted interchange of words possible. I have driven cabs where the glass screen *runnel stop*, which is removable, had been taken out by a naughty driver. Now the entire area is available to be opened as the glass doubled up on itself. The trick is to leave the partition in place and passengers do not realise it can be opened entirely. Then wait for someone worthwhile talking to, open it fully and hold a decent chat.

I drove long days choosing to work only two nights a week Friday and Saturday. My wife insists I live a normal life at least five days per week. Hence my weeks' work consists of four days and two nights. Winters I average a 40-hour week, summers as there is more money to be earned, I do 50 hours per week. To be precise I tried a variety of combinations of day and night work.

Nightfall sees the transformation of places such as Soho (London's Mad Square Mile), from a colourful meeting place of the nations, to London's entertainment centre. As dusk approaches the crowds with children and aunts disappear and the area metamorphoses ready for sensation hunters and gourmets. There is snarling as the last remaining parking spots are struggled for and no stopping place is empty for more than seconds. About this time of day, the shoppers abandon the open-air markets and record shops. Now the waiters set the tables and polish glasses, welcoming in the first of the night's patrons hoping that the tables will be used more than once this same night.

While the police are busy radioing the positions of illegally parked cars to be towed away the crowds of sensation seekers move in. Everyone dressed in their best: men in sharp (or is it 'cool' today?) clothes, women's hair perfectly arranged, all sport teeth, sparkling with each laugh. Queues in front of the cinemas grow longer. Weekend drivers incite cabbies to blasphemy. Great fun is had by all. Hurrah for Soho! In the 21St C.- Covent Garden is not the only challenge for being 'the hub'. Meanwhile cabbies, doing on the spot U-turns, cause fright to non-Londoners out for the evening. Later around 20:00 the theatres are all 'On the Burst', and the out-flowing hoards are meeting the incomers for the second performance.

Now Trafalgar Square's resident pigeons and starlings begin seeking their night spots. Wheeling and whirling, they circle again and again until abruptly settling into the trees. It is no longer possible to see the individual leaves as there is so much settling and resetting. Their shuffling amongst the foliage does not stop their high-pitched cawing from filling the air. Who is making the most noise, the crowds thronging the square or the feathered visitors? The ornamental fountains, a renowned landmark for sightseers and avian visitors alike, light up one after the other.

This did really happen to me "Driver, you really must speak to me in your cockney accent - it has a wonderful sound, we had a maid from Battersea she had a darling accent, we used to admire her for it". I had a problem, educated as an evacuee in Hove, my Sussex accent was not acceptable.

This group of elite punters were living in a forgotten world, which existed before WWII. Today a diminishing number of Cockneys are in the trade. Indeed, a number of drivers commute in from suburbs or dormitory towns. Others have left their previous workplaces and decided driving is more lucrative, and or, less stressful than previous occupations. On the other hand, I heard of a cab driver who left the trade because he did not like people talking behind his back.

I suppose in most people's minds there lurks an archetype of London Cab Driver. The picture may vary from person to person but basically it is the same. The pattern was set up in the Victorian era when the cab drivers with their 'Growlers' (a four wheeled horse drawn cab) were a much-maligned group and perhaps then justly so.

Today (1962) part of that image persists with the cab driver demanding "That's 'arf a crown Guv". If you need change, he will have it secreted in his undermost waistcoat – the last of three but he will first have to penetrate his oversized overcoat. This does in fact hark back to the old days, for cabs were and have always been so draughty that an overcoat was necessary to wrap round your ankles to keep the cold away. There are still drivers who talk about the old days, when cabs had no windscreen and then a half screen, and finally a windscreen with wipers.

In some countries all it takes to be a cab driver/owner, is for the driver to buy his badge, and he can become a cab driver. Obviously, the Public Carriage Office is a more efficient method of controlling the trade. We in London can rank-up wherever the mood takes us, while it is common in many countries for cab cooperatives to buy a 'station'. Some cab companies abroad have several ranks, others just a single 'stand'. I have found a great deal of frustration in my dotage, on holiday in Eastbourne Sussex, to discover cabs will not stop when hailed on the street. Then, having ordered a cab on the phone having to wait up to 40 minutes while empty cabs fly past me without stopping.

For my own amusement, I am adding:

3d *Joey*
6d *Tanner (alternatively Bender)*
12d *Shilling, Bob*
2/6d *Half a crown, Tosheroon*
£25 *Pony*

All of this is spondulix (money).

Chapter 4
My Working Habits and The Battle for Punters

In those days, I could remember the sequences of the jobs, and could relate to my wife the pickup and set down points not to mention the fare and the tip. I did not get home to eat precisely at 20:00, but only when I was reasonably near to home, did I return. Although this was difficult for my spouse, this is the only sensible way to work, so she became accustomed to me arriving before the meal was ready and sometimes long after it was prepared. Later in my career we were sufficiently affluent for me to dive into the nearest Chinese and be gone some 20 minutes later, this meant I gained travel time not driving home and out to work again. I used to choose whichever Chinese or Indian I wanted.

Primarily I worked only at night, for it is more lucrative than day work, as we were by now really short of money. Nights paid better, for not only is there more work about, but it can be completed three times faster than during the day giving much more time to look for jobs. Oh yes, the meter does run faster at night.

My trusty bicycle was stolen, and I used to clamber onto my new 2nd hand Lambretta to start work about 17:00 and finish around 02:00 or 03:00. The best nights were Friday and Saturday. Friday was not only pay night, but many people went away or home for the weekend. Saturday is the night for going out on the town. Midweeks were pretty dull, and I used to cruise round a set sequence of streets in Soho and Mayfair whose routes were not too dissimilar from my 'West End Rambles'. Many residents were carless, and restaurant goers popping up out of the woodwork – and all was well.

While on the Knowledge I looked healthy, for we had a fairly good summer during which I was constantly tempted to spend the day lolling on the grass in Green Park instead of puffing round London on my push bike. A few weeks of night work saw a change. I quickly had the pallor of a night worker with dark rings under my eyes.

Soon my left-hand pockets wore out and were patched together with a colourful variety of available materials. I discovered they were not designed to carry loads of change and be dived into every couple of minutes. I was told that the banks would supply bags designed to carry coins and could be used without wearing out – I still have one. I continued to wear my seven-foot scarf which became grimier by the day. I am sure that my left arm grew by two inches from stretching out to receive payment for the trip, and from having to extend it to twist the clock downwards. Those were the days when the clock/meter was mushroom shaped (like the letter 'T') and had to be moved through 180 degrees to turn it on. It was actually in the space above the luggage platform, and I had to reach out to it, to start it running.

After work my homewards bound Lambretta journey was broken, only on the Chelsea Bridge Coffee Stall where I had a hot pie and drink. I joined the other late-night diners standing alongside the parked bikes, cabs and cars, all of us homeward bound. For me this last touch of the damp rising from the Thames and the rain was worth it. I was nearly home. I did not want to start cooking when I arrived home, all I wanted was to climb into a warm soft bed. Another pleasure was our cat 'Kimmie' who waited for me in the street and joined me on the climb up the stairs and into the flat.

One night many years on when we lived in Chiswick W4, I could only park at the bottom of the road, as every house's road parking space was full. I locked up and started to trudge homewards carrying my bulky bag. I must have looked suspicious and before long a police car stopped me as it was in the wee hours. My bag contained a torch, an empty snack box and my bank bag full of small change. We exchanged pleasantries and bade one another a friendly Good Night and continued on our ways.

Driving a cab is simple, finding a punter is more difficult and during the cold wet winter nights while scouring a neighbourhood it is not unknown to come to a road junction with four empty cabs facing one another. When this happens to me, I realise that streets in all directions have been covered only seconds ago. This means that I must now drive slowly along one of the streets recently searched, hoping someone will pop out of a restaurant, club, or house. It seems to be pointless when there is nary a person to be seen.

A similar situation happens when the empty taxi in front of me is not being driven at 30mph but cruising more slowly. I must now check whether it is the last in a procession of empty cabs, or alone. If alone, I could overtake him, but not pick up a fare if I see one on the next strip of road. This is where esprit de corps comes in, I would never break the unspoken code of etiquette and pick up a job that he would have had, if I had not overtaken him. When kerb crawling, and empty cabs abound, the only sensible solution is to put on to a rank and nod off. There are on those nights, too many drivers competing for too little work. Putting on a rank, there is always the possibility that someone approaching a rank will be picked up by a prowling cab, before he or they get to the rank. On the other hand, a rank is often next to a hotel, restaurant or club.

At night, in this sort of situation, the only persons who seem to be moving on foot are policemen. I was often tempted to ask one of them if I could give him a lift, but I never dared, desperate as I was for a job. I have long grown out of that thought, as I became more experienced, and realised he must continue on his lonely patrol, and I on my solitary vigil.

In the bad old days of the 1930s when cabs could wait several hours for a job, road surveys would show that out of every 100 cabs that passed in Oxford Street 90 were empty. It is said that drivers would give a 'Ha'penny' to kids, to ride in the back of the cab into a railway station. There the driver would be in a good position to filch a job without waiting hours on the official lengthy station ranks.

After midnight there are less conventional persons moving around. Those out on the street are certainly mysterious, gliding from shadow to shadow and the conventional London suddenly seems like toy town. This is where the action is. The Knowledge studies of streets in no way prepared me how to interact with this level of society. Was it reasonable for me to be searching here for jobs? I did not know if I was to be involved in a crime, or indeed subject to crime. The vehicle design in the early 1960s left the driver vulnerable. But half of the post-midnight custom was in dubious neighbourhoods. Everywhere else was dead still. I drove on, searching and searching the dark mysterious streets.
My imagination runs wildest in the ill lit neighbourhoods like Ladbroke Grove or Cable St. The yellow lit roads and grimy streets are quickly and efficiently deprived of lonely pedestrians as they enter houses or

hail cabs. Only novel writers of those years like Colin McInnes could interpret what I was looking at. He would conjure up a story of what was happening. In one brief moment, a person exits one building enters the next. A taxi deposits a couple, yet they go to different doorways. Movement is fast and flurried. A sudden precipitation of rain makes the lonely streets emptier than ever, but everything shimmers and glistens under the streetlights. The taxi and its driver reign as scavengers of the lonely pavements again and again, restlessly clearing them of people until dawn breaks.

An endless search was sprung on me by one of my passengers for an elusive friend. It drove me to despair, "Go there", "Let's try here", "Last stop there". I began to become disheartened, for the rider could well disappear at the next location. The only signs of people were house parties overflowing upwards from basements onto the sidewalk. The dull gloomy streets round about waited tensely for the situation to explode into something noisier enveloping the tenements round about. Luckily, I was quickly paid off and nothing untoward happened while I was present.

Later in my career I learned that when tourist numbers increased it was no longer necessary to trawl that type of district. Spring is the start of visitors to our city, and London's economy waits. Airliners from the world over arrive, and each year, they discharge strangers who manifest the same idiosyncrasies as last year's holiday makers. Two, three or even four weeks is not long to explore a country, let alone a continent, as some transatlantic travellers try. With foreign currencies and language to cope with, it is little wonder that local customs tend to be ignored. The climate is different, food and accents unusual. These in turn, can bring out and accentuate the visitors' national traits and behaviour which the incomer did not realise he possessed. As they are the antithesis of local custom, they disconcert cab drivers.

Every year, the street photographers and the buskers seem to have a foreknowledge of spring and appear along with the fresh sunshine, acting as harbingers, proving to me that "The seasons they are a changing". Businesses and residential streets remain unmoved, ignoring the new green shoots of natural Spring growth. but tradesmen including the shoeshine boys, show their acumen. They are for me, indicators of a potential boost to the number of clients that will soon be materialising.

Next in the year, in the summer months, sitting at home, I will hear the ice cream vans playing their tunes to entice children into the street to buy their wares, and I think of the Pied Piper.

Sometimes the pressures of time and speed common to some businesses also appeared to apply to tourists in London. So, I was not surprised to be stopped by a young woman from America who was quite out of breath. Between gasps for air, she asked for Madame Tussauds Waxworks. Off we set, and I, sensing that she was in a hurry, drove at top speed. While we were caught by a red traffic light, I discovered she had just come from the 'Changing of the Guards Ceremony'. She told me that she had enjoyed it and was overawed with the tradition that is our British heritage. At the next red lights, she enquired if I knew where Herbrand Street was, I replied that I did, and asked her what time her tour of London began?

Her reply confounded me. In an hour's time!! It was my turn to gasp. I asked no more questions and concentrated on my most efficient driving. It took me, who was born in London, one year doing nothing else but to discover all the nooks crannies, squares, monuments, gardens and roads, and here was this girl trying to see London in one day. We arrived at Marylebone Road, she paid me off and I slowly relaxed and calmed down.

Her mode of seeing London may have appeared hectic, but to my mind it was a good deal healthier than those of my passengers who enter the cab with cameras whirring and one eye closed. I then drive them round, stopping only when there is something of special interest and deserving an extra few foot of film. Some visitors' recollection of London must be a moving picture in a tiny square.

My qualifications to question transatlantic visitors might be queried. But I have a great deal of experience driving, perhaps a thousand incomers per year, identifiable by accent, hair, clothes, spectacles, and travel cases. Luggage labels are another give-away.

In 1962, in my London Style FX3 taxi, the suitcases sat next to me. Stickers often reveal names of travel agents from the visitor's country, a variety can indicate a well-travelled passenger. I carry professors, diplomats, soldiers, Madison Avenue executive types, students, post delivery men and more. Americans usually come from the East Coast, New York and New England, but once I had a fare from Hawaii. Some talk to me, some do not. 60 years after writing the above, my granddaughter is doing precisely this type of touring. Whirlwind sampling of what the world has to offer.

A mutual antipathy may be caused by factors on either side. Both of us think the other is brusque. The problem starts when I do not open the passenger door. The logic for me is, that there is a danger in opening my door and stepping out in front of passing cars. Traditionally, cabbies do not leave their seats unless they are in a side street and nothing is passing by. The second problem is that tourists behaving as they do at home enter the cab, and only when seated, give the destination. This is so easily done from the pavement and is the way 99% of English passengers give their destination. Sadly, once a passenger is inside, it becomes almost impossible to hear what the punter is saying (solved in the 21st century by speakers and inbuilt mikes).

The glass partition whilst preventing attack also acts as a sound barrier. If someone enters before relaying the destination, I have to crick my neck to confirm the address and plead for it to be repeated. Today that issue does not exist. However, what does happen now, is that the unwary passenger when speaking privately can be overheard by the driver.

I am frequently given the address in the following form which is admirable for its brevity - "28 Eaton", but this is London. We have Eaton Gate, Eaton Square, Eaton Place, Eaton Terrace, Eaton Mews, (North and South). All of these are in South West London. In North West London these names recur. Confusing, isn't it?

July 4, I remember the date, because my 4th passenger gave me a packet of popcorn and wished me a happy 4th of July. The morning started when a woman hailed me and asked to be taken to the "English Speaking Union". The pickup was Piccadilly which was a one-way street, and the building was behind us. Obviously, I had to drive with the traffic flow – forwards. I did so. We had not reached the first possible turn off before she started to scream that I was travelling in the wrong direction. She jumped out and would not listen to me. And ran off without paying.

The taxi door was still open, when a woman with her two daughters jumped in and asked for the Mount Royal Hotel. In less than 10 minutes the Hotel name blazing in red neon lights was in view when she decided to panic. She started to pound on the partition and said, "I want the Mount Royal Hotel". I wearily affirmed the address, and we arrived 35 seconds later. Four journeys later I was given the packet of popcorn, and I felt I was part of the human race again. Hurrah for Independence Day.

In my early days, I was unaware of how to recognise a drunk. That was soon solved. I either stopped before or after the would-be rider and watched his walk as he approached. Many is the man from whom I have roared away.

Sitting, waiting, on the various ranks I have listened to tales from veteran drivers and believed half. Some drivers professed that they know in advance whether a fare will "Pay Well" or not. I have picked up many a punter who was ignored by the empty cab in front of me only to find that he indeed did "pay well". It is I believe, ineffectual to try and pick good or bad fares.

Out of trade courtesy, I was following an empty cab down Lillie Road Fulham SW6. I was really irked as he was sticking to 20 mph or less, but it was only half a mile or so before the road split, and I would be able to get away from him and travel at my cruising speed of 30 mph. Suddenly the cab in front of me fastidiously ignored a punter, even though he was clearly looking for all potential passengers.

I noted a well-dressed middle-aged man, nowadays named a 'suit', deliberately waving his arm in a signal for a taxi. I stopped and picked up. The job only went 1/9p and I received 4 shillings, a 133% tip. In other words, I would not have a better job all night, most likely all week, yet the other cab had blithely ignored it.

The paying in system in those days, was from the meter readings, the meter divided in the owner's favour in the following manner: The number of jobs, i.e., fall of clock plus the number of units recorded, that is the number of times the meter fare clicked up. Extras and tips were for the driver, which were and are, a vital part of any driver's income.

Yes, I had studied for a year, but no one had explained to me how to work or how to spot a good job. All I had learned was names and routes

37

and so I became the classic butter boy. I had never noticed cab ranks, and I certainly never knew which rank was a good rank. I had no idea when long distance railway trains arrived at which stations.

The fable is that good luck falls in the way of the beginner, and I suppose I had my fair share. Though in later life I noticed if I returned to the steering wheel after a period away, I spotted many fares which other drivers had not noticed, and the longer I was away the better the results. During my first weeks brandishing my shiny new badge, I found that traffic flow had no rules or logic. For no recognisable reason it became denser in specific areas. There actually was a true rush hour when many wanted to get home. No one had mentioned that to me. A little trick I developed was to look for work in areas not usually traversed by empty cabs, and many is the passenger who has stepped into my cab with the words, "That was lucky". Little did they realise it was my good luck too

Chapter 5
Conversations

A variable in the day's work and a source of interest, is the passengers and the way they behave. The very first action of a rider as he or she seats themselves is to close open windows or open closed windows. Next, they either close the partition window or leave it. When the window is closed, I realise I am not part of their journey and ignore their presence concentrating on arriving at the destination as quickly as possible.

Those who do engage in conversation somehow or other, either finish up philosophising on life, or express attitudes coping with the world's problems, the economy, foreign wars, or any other matter in the headlines. Having discussed the evils of the economic situation and having arrived at the destination, we separate, agreeing on our conclusions. Both of us intent on our next purpose.

I suppose as a last resort or perhaps as a second round of expanding our conversational horizons, a passenger related to me that he was a journalist. That actually was sufficient for me to hold my words and leave well alone. After all, there was the tip to be considered. Sometimes stipulations crop up. There are some who explain they are short of money, others have a situation to be resolved, there are invalids, and now and again the journey is a race against time, i.e., a 'Hurry Up' job. Tourists frequently enjoy hearing tales of London. Some punters enter with an innate distrust of taxi drivers, whilst others settle relaxed and rely on the driver's integrity from the start.

In my early days, and still now, I am complimented on my road craft and route taking. It does not take much experience to know which of two or three lanes is fastest. At some point ahead there will be the turns at the junctions. I react well before we reach them. I have been asked if I trained in Paris or Brooklands or was trying to emulate Stirling Moss. Perhaps the greatest appreciation for my and other taxi drivers' skills was expressed to me during a dense fog which occurred recently. I was not surprised, for no one else would dare to go out in that sort of weather.

Very few motorists could drive or know where they were under those conditions.

The other night I really was showing off to some American passengers, and after I had made the cab do everything short of looping the loop outside their hotel, and swept with a final flourish, forwards to the entrance, when one of them leaned forward and said "Room 525, please!".

Once, I spent over an hour helping a young healthy, out of door type of girl, from Calabria Italy. I was approached at a station rank. I suspect the job had been brushed off a few times. She did not speak one word of English. I drove her to the correct railway station for her ultimate destination, there are 9 mainline railway termini in London. I helped her buy a ticket, showed her the platform and told her what time the train would arrive at her station, and luckily, we found someone who was going there too. I felt myself to be the logical responsible person to help, as I was able to communicate with her using my two dozen words of Italian.

On Tuesday, it was an Israeli who could not find an hotel room. London becomes super crowded during peak holiday periods. Following his suggestion, we left the centre and approached the suburbs and found a place in a more secluded area. He was so pleased that he gave me a large tip. This in turn pleased me, for I had been having a poor day's work, including a series of 'Legals', which are fares with no tip.

Often when there is a choice between a 'single pin' and a two or three hander, I opt for the crowd, for the extras (charge per person) would add my day's takings. The boss does not see this money. Luggage, as well, is an additional income for drivers. Journeys between midnight and 06:00. have a surcharge of one shilling (1/-, a bob in real money). This is not a great sum, compared to the time and a half that other night workers receive. Of course, *we are not obliged* to work evenings and nights.

Socially, I feel that there is a stigma attached to being a taxi driver, this might be a personal quirk, but I think many drivers feel as I do. Cabs seem to be picked upon by the constabulary. I am so much more at ease when I enter a cafe with no badge dangling from my lapels and no taxi key in my pocket.

Early one morning sitting outside the hotel on the Charles Street W1 rank which leads into Berkeley Square I allowed myself to daydream. Probably it was because I had only been awake for a couple of hours, and was daydreaming till something happened. Half a mile from the nearest underground station and bus stop, the flow of the walking public streaming to work seemed to engulf the cab. I felt the cab floundering against the tide. Swarms of persons passing on both sides of the road. Wave after wave of bobbing bowlers mingling with fashionable and not so fashionable female headgear, all floating on the crest of the flow.

They surged forward in battle order. Sometimes the black bowlers predominated, and I wondered if the City had lost its monopoly. And now a strong current of females dressed and groomed to win the war of the sexes. They crammed the pavement. I was in a minority. I was sitting motionless and everybody else was rushing forwards. I felt out of place. Some might have been in the West End for personal reasons, shopping or trysts but even so, they were part of the unceasing relentless tide swarming forwards to get to work on time.

Would an 'Airport job' come out of the hotel? My thoughts pirouetted. I recalled a young woman ingenuous enough to thank me for not swearing at her. She was in the wrong, and was surprised that I was not irate. It started at the traffic lights when I was waiting for the green light to appear, and was wondering what would happen if all the lights in London stayed red as long as this one. The very thought filled me with delight, and I decided I would be able to cut down my 11 mph average daily speed to 6 mph or even 5 mph I would actually slow the tempo of my life without departing from London. I was rudely awakened from my reverie by a lurch and simultaneous bang. I knew precisely what had happened. I had heard about this. This was a case of "I was sitting at the lights waiting for them to change when...". I jumped out of the cab quickly, alarmed only at the thought that I might lose potential witnesses. Ignoring the unhappy lady and her car – after all she was too close to my taxi to drive away. I pounced on the driver of the nearest car. "Your name and address Sir" I demanded ferociously. The sudden bang and the sight of a heavily over-coated figure charging at him like a wounded Hippo unnerved him. "Who, me? I ain't done nothing!". "I know that, but I must have your name and address as a witness, I know you are not responsible". Having obtained that information, I let him go. He was most relieved. I now turned to the girl:

"Let's swap cards and exchange car numbers".
"Aren't you annoyed?" she said fearfully.
"It's too late now the damage is done". I could afford to be magnanimous. I had my witness – I was surely in the right.
"Thank you again for not swearing at me, do you think I will be able to drive it away?"
With a professional eye I glanced at her vehicle. "I do not see why not, but not too far as the radiator is beginning to leak."
We said goodbye and I drove back to my garage.

Then, after explaining the incident to my boss, I had an enjoyable job for the next half hour: completing the Insurance Accident Report Form. This document stated at the very start, that dashes are not accepted, and all answers must be worded. Question: Age of third party? I really did not notice. Question: The weather? I wrote overcast and very cold. The Policeman's number. There was not one, so I answered Zero. Which Hospital? There was not one, so I added: Nowhere. Draw a plan of the accident. I marked the young lady's car embracing the cab, and when it came to a description of the collision, I extended my literary style and trusted my boss would not fire me for frivolity. Still, here I am still playing with words, 1962 till 2024, and I am at my age, no longer tense waiting at red traffic lights.

Chapter 6
More Conversations

Driving anything up to 100 miles a day in Central London, I break the monotony of round and round we go, by carrying on conversations with passengers. The opening gambit is often about the weather, then there is a progression to the sad state of the traffic - congestion. That leads into any current London event which adds to the driving misery, and then there is an inevitable final corollary to the talk "...they will have to do something about the traffic". We Londoners live on the verge of chaos and at least half of it is related to traffic (written 1963). Has anything changed (2023)?

To stimulate conversations which usually promote a good relationship with the passengers, I occasionally throw out a provocative remark or question asking their opinion on a new building. Alternatively, do they have an opinion on the new Stag Building which looks into the private grounds of Buckingham Palace? This can bring an interesting response. Occasionally, I encounter someone who is directly involved, such as an architect, engineer, or a real estate agent.

The best story heard for a long time, was that the new Vickers Tower on Millbank, which had recently become a well-known London landmark, was shifting on its foundations. Was the proximity to the Thames the cause of this rumour? There is today (2023) talk of converting the tower into apartments and an hotel. A similar story was told to me about the London Hilton Hotel, and it seems to me, it is possible that these tales are related in bouts of malice. An engineer said to me that for every million pounds spent on these massive buildings, one person involved in construction work will die on the site! I trust that this is no longer the case.

I find challenging remarks to suit the run. So once, I commented that the South African Embassy on Trafalgar Square was showing tins of pineapple in its windows. Three years previously, at the height of the boycott, to exhibit anything would have been foolhardy and obviously counterproductive. But since then, so much has changed. At that time, to show a product from S.A. which was to be sold in the shops would not have worked. I had hardly driven a couple of hundred yards before my passenger told me that he had recently returned from there and gave me a run down on what he had seen and experienced, and what he thought was going on. A few questions supplied other information. His personal views shone a different light on what the press was regularly reporting.

Once, when I talked of the demonstrations outside the new American Embassy in Grosvenor Square, it led on to the political bluff and counter bluff proceeding across the world. Today named *misinformation*. I discovered that my fare was stationed in Berlin, and had returned only yesterday from representing the United Kingdom at an international conference.

This question-and-answer game can lead to predicaments. Driving along, I enquired from which state of Australia my passenger came. My passenger was a most eloquent wife of an Australian Immigration Official and she was able to quash all the arguments I could raise for remaining in London, rather than emigrating to Australia. I explained I was a parasite living off the needs of Londoners and not contributing to London. Nevertheless, she was so convincing, I nearly became an Oz.

On another journey when I pointed out the M.R.A. Headquarters, I was given a fifteen-minute indoctrination into the necessity of moral rearmament. The pair of us were so involved that the rider nearly left without paying.

"Are you on holiday?" is another way to promote a response. This can lead on to "Have you been to the theatre?" Should the response be yes, we are away. One of my punters really flabbergasted me for he had visited nearly every theatre in town. I was out of my depths, for the man did not appear to be such a frivolous bloke. We fell into a discussion about the theatre and the merits of the various performances. Ultimately, I was vindicated, I had got it right. It turned out that the man was on the Watch Committee of his hometown in the North of England, and his drab demeanour suited his task of criticism. His critique matched his appearance and he appeared to me to be exceptionally biased, being both antiquated and intolerant of the sixties. As a Londoner, and having seen many of the productions myself, I decided his reviews were narrow minded.

Putting on either Earl's Court or the Olympia Exhibition Halls, I was sure to receive an answer if I enquired as to whether the show was any good. The response would keep me in touch with current trends and the Ideal Home exhibits would be described, whether I wanted to hear about them or not. The more professional the rider, the better the critique, and the information of the trends towards current Italian or Scandinavian designs. A follow on is of course, whether the attendance in the hall was high or low and how this would affect future sales. The Farmers' Show, and indeed the Motor Show or the Boat show, were equally a source of banter. The demonstrators and sales staff have equally interesting details to recount if they are not busy trying to sell me something I do not need, like the latest model Jaguar.

One of the more interesting passengers recently was the Reverend Hopkinson, who was a religious adviser to the ITV. He hailed me one day and asked me to drive him to the Old Bailey. I did not know who he was, but I did know that the Lady Chatterley case was being held there. He was flustered, for it seemed he was late, and it made me think that he was perhaps to appear there as a witness. I was correct. He said he understood that his relationships with his associates were in jeopardy, but he was obligated to say what he believed. He had only something to lose by his utterances but felt he must express what he believed. We had an intriguing neo-religious discussion while I drove at top speed through the congestion. He spoke on behalf of the book and ignored repercussions for speaking with freedom and sincerity. That journey and the conversation brought the trial to life for me.

Another uniformly interesting though not newsworthy character, was a Scotsman in service to a family in Sussex. He told me of his attitude to life, and this mainly covered his relationship with his employer. He explained that if he or his wife had a cold, they feared to relate it to their employers. Yet if the owner of the estate or his wife had a cold or a headache a great fuss had to be made of it. The man who looked bright and cheerful accepted this as the way of things and enjoyed life contentedly yet not smugly. He held no rancour for his employers, cannily letting the ill thoughts pass him by. He recounted only a feeling satisfaction with his status.

Employees acceptance of their position in society differs, some are self-centred in the extreme. Others have a message which they want to put over, some make good conversations, others are frightfully boring. A fascinating central point, and if I consider it, applies to me, is that the vast majority begin their thinking from an egocentric point of view, with the individual as the centre point. His or her life is inside a tiny circle, within a larger circle embracing the nuclear family, then comes the circle of relatives, blood, and in laws, and so forth until the very last and most nebulous circle contains humanity and the universe. Even persons with a highly moral sense of propriety will ignore the largest and furthest perimeter, if push comes to shove.

When there is a lack of communication between myself and the passenger I take note of their behaviour – for want of any other diversion. The average person drops into the passenger seat with a thud that rocks the vehicle, and it is rarely that I have to turn to see if the rider is seated. If either of the passenger windows is open the cigar or cigarette smoke blows through my cabin before leaving the vehicle, and I always know when a lady or gentleman is dousing him or herself with perfume before leaving the cab and I imagine that a romantic meeting is about to begin.

Among the number of people I talk to, the amount that winter abroad is amazing. I have only to mention the winter rain or slush to obtain the comment "Oh I never see that, I am usually in Italy". From there the discussion continues revealing that their real home is in Scotland, but they are often in New York, and are at this time just passing through London to shop or are en route to a foreign destination. These persons whose incomes must be way above the average are perhaps nouveau riche, perhaps they are the traditionally wealthy. I rarely am able to guess to which group they belong.

"Have you been shopping?" This conversation opener once promoted a unique rejoinder. "They have been putting the flags out for me!". Not quite understanding the meaning of the words, for the man was a lithe octogenarian, I was not quite sure whether he might have a sprightly imagination to match. Then he continued relating that the flags were outside the Royal Academy. I was impressed the more so, as he continued, that he was exhibiting 60 years of painting on over 300 canvasses. Only the next day perusing the papers while waiting on the Sloane Square rank, I discovered I had driven Russell Flint and that there was an exhibition in his honour in the Diploma Gallery.

Chapter 7
Private and Public Life

Recently, I started to wonder why I ask all these questions, for I am by nature not inquisitive and was brought up not to intrude into private matters. I traced this back to my early days of driving. When we went to visit socially, and it became clear that I was a genuine black cab driver, everyone became excited and began to quiz me. Whilst a modicum of questions were about techniques and ethics, it appeared that a large number of our acquaintances had never met a cabdriver socially. Everything, short of my bank balance was asked about driving a taxi.

Can a driver work from anywhere in London? Do you work a particular area? What hours do you work? Is it worth your while owning your own cab? Why, do cabs not stop when I hail them? Why don't you want to go south of the river? The questions seemed to be endless, and there was always a story about personal experience where the drivers' behaviour was questionable, and there was always a good laugh to be had. Perhaps this happens to others no matter what their trade or profession.

Nowadays not driving a car, or a taxi, I find myself riding in a taxi as a passenger, I enjoy the ride and generally know which route the driver will take. There are times when I specify which route to take, on the other hand, I once let the driver make a major error which cost me a shilling as I somehow guessed he was lost or bewildered. The sheer luxury of sitting in a cab makes me feel good, and I find myself among the eccentric minority that keep their feet off the tip-up seat.

Sitting alone on a rank, sometimes I ignore the chatter opportunity taken by other drivers, I sit, perhaps reading a paper or book, sometimes pondering on the public's attitude to cab drivers. There were several ranks which I favoured because of the telephone: South Kensington SW7, Hampstead NW3, and particularly Sloane Square SW1, which was my nearest rank to home. Between the calls from the phone and the shoppers at Peter Jones Store, the rank 'ran' pretty well. Over the years due to the yobs tearing the fixtures off the phones, and the existence of minicabs, the phones fell into disuse. I remember a driver, his name was

D'Arcy, who used all his savings to replace the derelict phone at South Ken. Station.

One of the great attractions of taxi driving is the freedom to choose working hours. I am free to start and finish whenever I think fit. I can look for work anywhere I choose inside the Metropolis and even choose who I will or will not pick up. The choice is mine. Though obviously there are drawbacks. Since I enjoy a comparatively high standard of living, I chase myself to work hard. However, the temptation is constantly there to pack up and sit peacefully in the park daydreaming. The work might give the impression of repetition: search for a passenger, deliver the passenger and start again. However no two jobs are the same. I frequently feel obliged to solve my passengers' problems, for it is me who knows London best. Hotel rooms, railway stations, interesting restaurants, new exhibitions. I endeavour to find and bring my passenger to his or her desired destination. I accept a moral obligation to see he arrives once he has engaged my services. The feeling is stronger when I realise that my passenger is a tourist.

At that moment, I have the feeling I am the host, and as a representative of London I bear a responsibility to the visitor. Then, driving, I look at the City in the way I suspect a tourist might, seeing London for the first time. I try to look at the streets, people, architecture, the giant double decker buses, and prefer to disregard displays, and ignore neon advertisements, attempting to see London as a newcomer. Occasionally I see the detritus for what it actually is strewn haphazardly on the pavements and curbs, plastic coffee cups rolling in the wind competing with papers and feel ashamed for the metropolis. Then later the shame turns to dismay at the sad sight of rough sleepers huddled alongside shop windows. Perhaps London is not so grand.

There is yet another manner of regarding London which I experience when bringing a Londoner back to his home after a holiday. I see London in a different light again. Or to be precise, I look at his local area, his neighbourhood, with different eyes. I try to see it as he must. His local high street and his shops, his 'Pub' his own street and house. The streets now lose the dull anonymity which passers-by ignore of dull soulless lengths of tarmac with duplicated homes on either side. But for the returning Londoner light standards erectly lining the roads' perimeters, can perhaps hold the significance of years of acquaintance.

They become alive with his memories and his experiences. Finally, I am told to stop alongside a yellow hedge guarding a recently created car parking place outside his home where his garden used to be.

I am frequently alarmed at the way old vistas are spoiled with new brash constructions which serve Mammon. Other times I am inspired with recently erected fountains, monuments, and statuary. Memorials that are again revealed when washed clean of decades of grime, and now spotlight in the night sky return to be pleasant sights. The best time of day is when a pink sunset delineates the tops of the structures as black silhouettes against a rosy firmament at the end of clear summer's day. Now for the next 15 minutes, one by one, the tower buildings' windows begin to show their yellow lights and new asymmetrical patterns replace the skyscraper's austere darkness.

The attitude of rider to driver is mostly rational, that of boss to employee. At times it can be galling to be the subservient (ha-ha) driver. Sometimes that overwhelming superiority is infuriating, especially derision, and I have time and again had to explain that if the driver were master of manners and logic, he would not be driving a taxi. There is another attitude by the timid occasional rider, and that is of fear. Some passengers will go to any length to avoid a harangue.

The stress, first time or occasional riders have, occurred the other night at the 'Vic' (Victoria Station to you). I leaned out of the window and said "Madam" to a pair of women as they approached my cab. Without pausing, they turned away to the cab behind me. I shouted out to them that I had only said" Madam". I guessed then, what had upset the women: they had had enough, and did not want a scene. Presumably the moral cab drivers behind me had said "Not me, the one in front", in order to honour the queue system, and by the time they had paraded the length of the queue, they were 'trained' to move onwards. It was a little chaotic at that moment inside the station, with some drivers arriving and immediately picking up rather than joining the long line of waiting cabs. Possibly other drivers had honourably declined picking up the ladies as the drivers had not waited on the rank.

I have experienced a fellow driver literally attempting to pull a five hander out of my taxi, after the man of the party decided that he would lose his dignity and air of 'man about town' if he were directed to yet one more cab departing from the station following the one-way system, I was apprehensive that another cab driver would lean out of his window and shout "What's the matter? Hungry?" as if I had nicked a job.

I had a friend who had a bit of a temper, and this was while we were driving the FX3 taxis, which would sometimes have to be wound up with a starting handle. We all learned how to do this the hard way: swinging the handle keeping one's thumb together with the fingers. This was because the motor would sometimes kick back (backfire) and bring the handle back onto your thumb if it was separate from your fingers, and so causing a sharp pain, as the metal cracked onto the bone.

My friend for some reason drove a cab which frequently cut out. I presume it had a dodgy battery, and he had to wind it up so often that he kept the starting handle handy next to him in his driver's cabin. The only trouble was that if he became really angry, he would grab the handle and threaten the errant passenger. The PCO heard of this, and he was warned off for having an *offensive weapon* with him. He was asked to leave the starting handle in the boot with the spare wheel. Luckily nothing worse happened. He eventually gave up taxi driving and trained as a social worker!

Though we are not the personification of wisdom and manners, we do accept some of the onuses which the job entails. One Cup Final night shortly after midnight, a party of Greeks fans approached me and politely asked for an hotel not too far from where they hailed me in Bayswater. When we arrived, they did not like the look of the place. I then accepted one of the heavier responsibilities with which I sometimes saddle myself, that is finding accommodation for visitors on holiday. I did not appreciate what would follow, when I agreed with their impression that that the hotel was not the most salubrious and consented to help them to find another. Their air of jubilation from the football result had not died out, and they relied on me to solve the hiccup. We tried 8 or 9 hotels in the area. All were full, and then we found a manager with a kind heart who though he did not have rooms, phoned around to hotel after hotel, as I suggested them, to no avail. It then occurred to me that there was one last chance. So, we drove to the relatively expensive Great Western Hotel at Paddington, and one hour after they had first hailed me, we obtained the last two rooms there. It was one of those occasions where I had to forfeit the potential work which would have been available on a Cup Final night for the basic responsibility of being a cab driver.

The way pedestrians hail cabs sometimes indicate their nationalities or manners. I have had a hand clap used to stop me. It has to be loud for me to respond. Some use the 'Will you stop and give me a lift' sign I used while hitch hiking throughout Europe. There are locals who think they are clever and whistle like we are dogs and wait for us to respond.

The layabouts whistle and then ignore me as I stop, and I begin to wonder if I had imagined the noise. The most accepted City signal is to brandish a furled umbrella. The raised arm, the flagging down sign the type which is used on animals: "down boy, down". Now and then it upsets me.

The umbrella which is effective during the day is useless at night, as the black umbrella is invisible against a black sky. Doormen pump their oversized rain covers up and down, making a show of it to impress the would-be passenger. I have even been hailed by a slightly elevated eyebrow. There are those who hail me and having caught my eye, immediately look away, leaving me to wonder if I was imagining the movement.

Frequently, I have nearly passed someone on the pavement before I am hailed. This is because the would-be rider cannot see if I have someone in the rear of the cab. In the summer they are wearing dark coloured glass lenses. They grope their way into the cab and at the end of the journey ask, "How much is on the clock?". Ultimately, they give in and remove the shades so they can see how much they are paying me, the more so at night in the darkest neighbourhoods. High fashion is abandoned for a brief moment.

The following paragraph is of its time:

A woman will hail me, and then as soon as she has seen that I have changed direction and am approaching her and is certain I will stop, she will look away. This is all part of the sex war, and she does not want to warrant any extra attention from the driver. Aware of her attraction she lowers the possibility of an awkward exchange. On the other hand, it is possible that realising her beauty she is helping the vehicle not crash as the driver's attention wanders!

Occasionally I have been graded 'unmanly' by elderly punters who expect me to risk my life in Knightsbridge traffic. They want me to jump out and stand alongside the Harrod's doorman. I have in a most serious and earnest manner been told to jump out of the taxi to walk round it and pick up a fallen glove. The explanation was, I had complied with a superstition. There are young women who by sleight of hand introduce luggage into the passenger compartment – keep it out of sight not paying the extras. On arrival expect me to carry it to their front door forgetting they had carried it to the cab and lifted it in all with no effort.

A Taxi is an obvious removal van for hire. The punters moving home were often embarrassed using the taxi to transfer their possessions, until I told them that I was used to it. Fridays and Saturdays, people change digs, packing their travelling cases into the cab and ensuring their paraffin stoves are in an upright position so that no paraffin spills, some stoves were still warm from recent use. Next comes washing up bowls full of odd and ends. Then blankets, all to be crammed into the taxi. Many have their own T.V. sets, some have odd pieces of furniture, and it is possible to see how far they have progressed in the great rat-race. Now and then people upgrade their accommodation, and I feel somehow that I am aiding them to improve their lives. Most often the moves are from like-to-like accommodation.

Frequently asked for assistance often in minor removals from flat to flat, I not only aid the person but actually save myself time by doing so. About a year ago I was called to a house in Highbury N5 and asked to wait while the woman brought out a parcel and then she returned to the house to bring another, and I realised that this was probably a moving job so offered to help. She was definitely not keen, but I followed her up the stairs to her tiny apartment motivated as much by curiosity as by masculine flourish. "Which room Miss?" She indicated a doorway. I boldly entered what was the smallest bedsitter I had yet seen.

To my chagrin, half of it was filled with a uniformed and be-helmeted police sergeant. Rather than be put out by this I quietly picked up two suitcases and a bag and retreated in a dignified manner. Perhaps this was one time when my help was superfluous.

Several years previous to this incident I arrived in Soho with a heavy woman who was asleep. We arrived in Old Compton Street W1 which was the destination. She later claimed she was genuinely asleep. As usual on a Saturday night no vehicles were moving, we were all, half gridlocked the only movement being the crowds swirling around looking for the most attractive venue. Wanting to dispose of my passenger as quickly as possible so that I could work my way out through the traffic, I attempted to wake her. I turned the powerful passenger lights on and off as my voice was insufficient to rouse her. Neither the illumination nor my bellows woke her. Seeing that no vehicle was moving I jumped out of my seat. By now a friendly crowd had gathered and were shouting advice and volunteering to help us out. I clapped my hands in front of her face then shook her, pleased that there was a crowd to witness my orderly behaviour. Suddenly she came to, scowled and asked:

"What do you think you are doing?" "You are making a spectacle of me!". She spat out disgustedly "Turn off the lights and drive on to the destination".

"Yes" she said, "I am doing the show at the club tonight". Since then, pondering on the difference between 'Being made a show of' and 'doing the show'. I have come to the conclusion that perhaps she was right, and I was in the wrong.

One murky evening in Swiss Cottage NW3, I had left the cab to itself as I hauled the luggage of a very old and fragile couple to their front door, via the many steep stairs to their flat. When I returned to the vehicle SHE was there. Her black hair shining in the streetlights glistening as it flowed over her young shoulders. She fixed her Kohl encrusted eyelids upon me, and I shivered as she spoke her words in a husky voice that was barely audible against the street noises. "Do you know where the 'Witch's Cauldron' is?" If this Sybil did not know, how could I, a mere mortal, know that? Resisting more shudders, I replied in the negative. She turned, glided away silently with serpentine movements her hair floating after her. Locking the door not to be jinxed, I laughed at my fears.

Day drivers have different same problems to nightmen. Two friendly looking men appearing to be well dressed and intelligent climbed into the cab and said "So". He looked at me I looked at him. His expression changed from the quizzical, mine to the interrogative. I responded "So". He seemed pleased that I understood him and said "Soo". This time there was a subtle difference which my mental destination storage unit noted, I let my facial features relax as the word clicked into place then I spat out triumphantly "SoHo". Another challenge met and completed.

Nowadays, I do not pull up precisely where the would-be passenger is standing though I can do so easily. While at the Royal Society for the Prevention of Accidents I explained I was a cab driver. The man with whom I talked, told me one of the major faults of taxi drivers is stopping dead, and thereby causing a pile up of the following traffic. Now I always swing into the curb as far as obstructions will allow and stop gently. Sometimes this is not so easy when the passenger at the end of a journey is hammering on the window and screaming "Stop here cabby, you have already gone past it".

I had only just set down in St. James Square SW1 when I saw a fellow running at me full gallop. He was not travelling fast but was exerting a great deal of effort to cover the ground. He arrived at the cab puffing laboriously and could barely gasp out the destination. All the time I had been grinning broadly, for he seemed a merry sort of fellow and not likely to take offence. He asked why I was smiling, and I told him. Then he invited me out to supper on the basis of my good humour. I replied, "What are the conditions?" He responded there were none, but I could make my own. I declined the offer and he was offended, but I did not know what the outcome of the matter might have been. I have learned a lesson and do not smile so readily at an approaching fare.

There is a class of punter who will jump into the taxi without giving me the destination, sometimes they are from outside the UK. This could of course, lead to a breach of the antiquated Carriage Acts which control the taxi trade. For we are not obliged to accept journeys over six miles (1962). Tradition has it that the driver can charge double fare to cover the cost of the return journey. In the old days the nag would be worn out! There is an ambiguity in recent cab acts of parliament, which by the way, exist from 1831 onwards. The recent acts suggest that a driver may refuse a fare which is further than 12 miles. To me, this is not clear: 12

miles in one direction, or there and back 12 miles? There is a further clause which permits the driver to refuse a journey which takes more than one hour. Furthermore, there is a different set of regulations for cabs picked up at Heathrow airport.

Driving down the broad and dignified Whitehall SW1 late one night on my way towards Trafalgar Square, I was the only person in the only vehicle in this vicinity at this time of night. I felt almost regal and not a little lordly. Then I spotted a man, and what's more, he hailed me as he crossed the empty road between the solemn architectural monoliths of Ministries and Government Departments. I did not ignore him and stopped more or less on the spot to save us both travelling to the curb some walking distance away. Even as he began to tell me the address, I pulled inwards to the curb. He gave an address in Hampstead and told me his preferred route. Meanwhile the constable, guarding the entrance to Downing Street SW1 just off Whitehall, where The Prime Minister's and Chancellor's houses stood, strolled over and began to berate me for failing to start the clock. Starting the clock is a legal requirement that ensures insurance holds, but only after the destination is given, and accepted. I had not yet agreed to take the passenger.

This was in the days before barriers were erected to protect the PM, blocking access to Downing Street and one could easily walk into this vulnerable political target. The police officer had abandoned his post leaving the homes of two top people open to malcontents. He was probably bored – but who likes cabbies anyway?

After the policeman had left us, we continued northwards and I complained bitterly that recently, another policeman who had abandoned his post outside Sir Winston Churchill's home in Hyde Park Gate SW7, and went to Sir Winston's aid after he had slipped and had damaged his back was severely censured for leaving his post. It took Sir Winston himself to clarify the matter. However, it appeared more important to catch a taxi driver moving a few yards closer to the curb and talking to the fare, than to guard the present Prime Minister's residence.

Chapter 8
Minicabs

I became particularly interested in the public's attitude to cabs about the time that minicabs came into prominence. Obviously, there was something amiss in our house that needed sorting out. I had not yet realised that from its very inception the concept of *a minicab for hire* had unofficial support inside the Ministry of Transport. The law stated, and remains, that a car has to be previously booked before it can pick up on the streets of London. This obviously ensures that no pirate individuals can charge or do what they like. Every cab driver and cab are registered with the police, otherwise known as the PCO.

Uniquely, solely 'Black Cabs' can pick up on the spot. If Private Hire Cars were removed from the centre of London the present number of cabs would be incapable of bearing the extra workload of passengers wishing to be driven from A to B. There are certain facts which must irritate the public: the way we always seem to be going home whenever there is a need, generally about 17:00. After a tedious working day, individuals wishing to be driven home or to a restaurant find themselves informed that the driver is 'going home'. I usually manage to point the cab towards home via the bus route, but sure enough, would-be riders wait for buses on the wrong side of the road. It is most unfortunate we cannot seem to split our working day in any other manner. The day and the night men get a share of at least one rush per day. So, the change-over is 16:00, 17:00, 18:00. each day. There are many day-drivers returning homewards or to the garages where the night-man is waiting, the individual day-man would only be too pleased to earn an extra couple of bob or so. With the appropriate notification of the direction the cab is travelling, the driver could add to his daily takings. Writing this, I am aware that unscrupulous drivers could make such a plan untrustworthy. Hence the authorities have reason to doubt the probity of such a system.

With the arrival of minicabs on the scene, my gut reaction combined anger and frustration. We were skilled and tested drivers, driving highly expensive licensed vehicles which cost more than £1,000 each, now being supplanted by minicab operators. They were able to undercut our prices, with drivers, whose sole qualification was a driving licence. The vehicles they drove were the cheapest on the market and were not subject to an annual scrutiny such as we were. The vehicles were bought from Renault at a premium price. To add to this financial advantage, they were permitted to advertise on the door panels. It took many more years until taxis were allowed to display advertisements.

I recall an occasion when I called the attention of a policeman to the flapping jagged edge of a minicab. He willingly aided the driver in a temporary repair, rather than book him for driving a vehicle which was a danger to the public. I grimaced to myself thinking, what would have happened to me if I had the temerity to go on the road with a cab in that condition. This assistance typifies the attitudes prevalent through-out this period. Though the police would come down on us for any petty infraction of the law, they would permit blatant illegal plying for hire on the public highway. Their vehicles were emblazoned with signs announcing it was available to anyone who approached it. The legal trip was for the driver to radio his office confirming the *booking which had just walked up.* I have known cab drivers warned about plying for hire in an unauthorised place, in the middle of the night, when they have stopped the cab and approached an Oxford Street store window, and stared in at something they might buy, while a minicab was permitted to stand anywhere any time.

This growing scourge was jointly feared by the trades' union and cab companies. They amalgamated to fight for the livelihood of the drivers and the vast investments in cabs that fleet owners had expended. The 'Masters' were in a financial position to challenge the minicab proprietors at their own game. The Unions upon consideration realised that we were supplying a luxury service, and that even if we withdrew our labour, nothing much would happen.

The Trade Unions tried to make representations in the courts of the illegality of this system. The journeymen such as myself and the owner drivers combined to form a Crisis Committee which endeavoured to take these problems through the High Courts. The Committee consisted mainly of journeymen and Mushes, who had invested past and future savings in the purchase of cabs. Every driver had invested a minimum of one year in study and considered that The Green Badge was a guarantee of sole right to ply for hire on London's highways, and was not ready to yield that privilege without a fight. There was a tendency for the minicabs to work the suburbs, and often they squatted around or near underground stations catching the commuters en-route to or from work. They even opened local offices. In this manner a great deal of work was syphoned from the yellow badge drivers who worked the suburbs. That is one of nine sectors in the greater London Authority area. Today (2022) where I live in South Woodford, minicabs work the underground station and legitimate taxis work the supermarkets and restaurants a short distance further on.

An unending task was begun in the raising of funds to pay for counsel. For every case that was found in our favour, another two had to be fought to clarify a separate set of circumstances. The search for finances still goes on in 1962 while the minis (scabs) steadily consolidate their position. The Crisis Committee decided to close down, the lack of funds made the battle impossible.

A problem we had to face with minicabs, were the flashy adverts that covered the exterior of the minicab. Taxis are only permitted to advertise in specific places inside the vehicle. Without even taking passengers, the company was earning money. The counterbalance of this profit was a couple of private radio stations, they had to set up, one at Crystal Palace. In the days before mobile phones, the radio was a vital instrument in the role of their legal/illegal plying for hire. Pye radio was the transmitter. The minicab price known before the passenger started his journey was one shilling per mile driven.

Everything appeared simple. A member of the public would approach a parked red Renault Dauphin with the appropriate advertisements and request a destination. The driver would then contact the office which would authorise the journey, and in this manner the driver had not plied for hire. One of the anomalies which the company Welbeck Motors suffered from, was illegal parking fines. The drivers having chosen sites, which they thought might be lucrative.

But in all, it was actually left in the hands of individual drivers to take some action. Not possessing aggressive genes, I wrote to each and every company which used the sides of the minicabs to advertise its own products, saying that I thoroughly enjoyed their product but, in the future, I would refrain from buying the product as their adverts were threatening the demise of the cab trade.

A problem was that the gas and electricity companies were posting their products on the 200 plus Renault Dauphins. Undeterred by the size of the companies advertising I determinedly wrote to the commercial attaché at the French Embassy describing myself as a Francophile and taxi driver, who wondered why Air France through their advertising on the minicabs was trying to destroy the London Cab trade.

Reading my outgoing mail to the many companies that advertised on the minicabs it would have seemed that I was particularly affluent, for I threatened not to buy any product which was advertised on a minicab. I pretended I was in the process of carpeting a house, fitting a safety belt to my new car, buying five pairs of shoes and acquiring a new T.V. In point of fact the only articles I had from this list are 3 pairs of old shoes bought over a long period. I often wonder if this bout of literary invention was how my yen to write started.

Generally speaking, every taxi driver made life as difficult as possible for every minicab driver. Whilst the camaraderie between taxi drivers on the road in yielding to one another halves the difficulty in making a 'U' turn or changing lanes in dense traffic, it makes the driving day more tolerable. No cab however, yielded to a minicab. The general driving public behaved as usual, which meant it must have been tough to drive in London's maelstrom. Michael Gotla, the minicab entrepreneur briefed his drivers describing them as 'His Army'. Press reports mentioned "Gay Little Pirates".

These expressions increased the animosity which we felt at that time. Not only did we harry these drivers physically, but as one journalist put it, we "glared at them in a manner which was sufficient to make their tires shrivel". Rather late in the day 'The Crisis Committee' was formed because the Union claimed it was making a fight, but it became increasingly obvious that nothing was happening.

The Committee instigated a variety of initiatives, some were commercial, others were described in the courts as the work of agents provocateur. One of the most blatant and effective efforts, was our boycotting venues such as hotels which needed us many times a day.

The London Cab, a legitimate trader, was and is providing, specific places and venues with an irreplaceable service. Managements were made aware that we were part of their service. They had thought they could perhaps oust us, or would perhaps use cabs in conjunction with the usurping buccaneers.

A trial boycott was called at the Westbury Hotel Conduit Street in Mayfair. It only came to my notice when I tried to put on the rank, one which I favoured. I was waved away by a couple of men on the pavement. Suddenly the management of the hotel understood that there was a 24-hour service of licensed vehicles available 365 days a year. It did not take long before the Hotel comprehended taxis would not put up with the minicab nonsense. They mended their ways. If someone in the hotel wanted a minicab the hotel would not supply it.

A couple of nights later I returned to the garage around 22:00 when the cab washer told me the jubilant tidings that a successful boycott had been called at the newest and then most expensive hotel in London: the Carlton Tower on Cadogan Place SW1. I was told by the exuberant washer that there was a notice in the foyer that any employee calling a minicab would be dismissed on the spot. I was so excited that I thought a trip to the hotel, not so far from our Battersea home would not come amiss. Guessing my wife was appropriately attired, I rushed home and changed into civilian clothes, while asking her if she would come with me for a drink. She was more than a little surprised when after parking the cab we entered one of London's chic restaurants, The Rib Room. There we ordered Vodka and lemon which was reasonably priced at double the norm. As it was just before closing time, we had a second round which was a trifle more expensive. We sat and admired Topolski's cartoons and then we wandered through the Hotel admiring the murals he had created. We absorbed the general décor which though lavish, was not excessive. On the first floor we looked into the Chelsea Room where we decided to have one more drink. We sat and listened to the Muzak which we had both thought might be intrusive, but was so soft that we could talk sotto voce and easily hear one another. Yet if the conversation flagged there was a pleasant melody, in no way interfering with feeling of wellbeing.

The waiter arrived with the drinks and said, "You know these drinks are rather expensive Sir?" I smiled, for double the price is expensive but I did not care as we were in this rather luxurious environment. Then he told me the price, and these drinks were quadruple the usual price. I tried not to shudder and genially paid, feeling like a total ass. Later I found out that I was buying a drink out-of-hours and was paying for a non-existent sandwich. However, the purpose of the exercise was to see if it were possible to hire a minicab inside the hotel. On the way out I approached the desk clerk and asked," What would happen if I requested a minicab?"

He gave me an old-fashioned look and replied that he would be unable to call one for me, and advised that if I really wanted one, I should call from the nearest telephone box. He continued that he had suffered all day with clients lining the pavements trying to obtain taxis. I thanked him for the information and as we left the hotel the commissionaire asked if we wanted a taxi. I said no and bid him Good Night not daring to tell him I had *my own cab* round the corner. Since that night, I have seen no patrons of this Hotel using minicabs.

The general feeling was sufficiently bad for about 40 cab drivers to be prosecuted over this period. There were rallies, and on occasions some 2,500 Hackney Carriages blocked traffic in Central London.

When a court decision made it clear that a minicab parked on a street corner was indeed plying for hire the game was up, and by the end of 1962 there were no more pirate vehicles lining the streets of the city. They had launched on the 9 June 1961.

In order to make a profit, minicabs had to raise their prices which made them closer to ours. As their numbers diminished, they became more difficult to locate, and subsequently a profit for the individual companies became more difficult. There were even journeys where they were more expensive than ours - additionally so, as the driver frequently did not know the route let alone the shortest route, the extra miles recorded brought the price very close to ours. Then in those days, if you saw a man poring over a map while sitting in a dirty little beaten-up car you could make a safe bet, he was an unauthorised driver. The problems a new driver faced would be multiple. Primarily, to locate the pickup point, then to devise and memorise the quickest route to the destination. For us, the map of London was ingrained into our memories.

A blind man who spoke to me on a journey and explained that with the inauguration of the service he decided to use them. Until one day, he was as usual helped into the minicab by one of his employees. He normally travelled with his expensive radio equipment from work to home. Arriving there, his wife guided him out of the vehicle. That night wanting to listen to something, he discovered the absence of the gear. The minicab company when contacted maintained that they were not liable. He then threatened them with legal proceedings. They did not demur. It was only when he told them, that the RNIB. was poised to take action did they compensate him for the equipment. My punter declared that such an occurrence would never have happened with a licensed taxi.

I have revised these words in 2022, and though the book concerns the 1960s I have recently come across a piece I wrote in the interim. The long smouldering controversy which today involves the international organisation Uber, followed the late 20th Century period which gave birth to mini-police i.e., private security organisations, mini cars, minibuses, mini versions of supermarkets and many other forms of miniaturisation. There was even a period of unlicensed pirate radio broadcasting stations, which preceded today's official local programmes.

Modernisation does not let society or old customs of life stand still; there is a constant throb for progression, and the authorities combined with the wisdom of the legal professions have grudgingly acquiesced to an apparent public demand. The usage of smaller unlicensed cars was and is nigh on irresistible, in fact it succeeded. There was a period where in a hydra like situation, new mini cab firms multiplied. They existed on their own terms in every corner and adjacent to many suburban underground stations. In parallel, the order and control over the Hackney Carriage never wavered. But anarchy persisted with these new minicabs. In this period if one opened a telephone book in a kiosk, it was a simple task to discover a list of minicab firms as long as an arm, with the additional help of loose cards slipped into the phone book announcing that day's new minicab companies. Turn the page to Taxi, and the same cards would slip out not content with the block printed adverts at the top and bottom of the Taxi Cab page, blatantly designed to seduce the public from taxis the loose cards demanded attention. Consequently, they squabbled with other mini cab firms and tried to beat them at their own game.

When minicabs first came on the scene, the numbers could be counted on one hand, today there are innumerable firms. The manner in which Gotla's Welbeck Minicab Co. first appeared on the market, was unfortunate, as if almost designed to antagonise cab drivers, while attempting to create a customer base. Named 'Soldiers in a War', the minicabs were in some way supposed to give the public a different choice, allowing booking in advance, compared to waiting in the rain for a passing cab.

I hate to admit it, but the service provided by the now regulated and authorised firms, has slowly produced advantages which the London Hackney Carriage does not provide. It utilises computers which explain to everyone where a mini is and when it will arrive. It provides details of its progress across the Metropolis to anyone who wants to watch the safe transit of a person sent off.

One night returning from far afield we left Kings Cross Station, searching for a passing taxi. It was very late, and we were travelling with our children. In desperation we found a minicab and told him our destination. All went well in town where the vehicle did not gain much momentum and we told him the directions.

No sooner than we had left the traffic lights behind us and there were long straight roads ahead he was able to pick up speed. Then without my paying attention it became obvious that as we approached any cross traffic and traffic lights. He began to meticulously change down one gear after the other to slow the vehicle. I am sure he put his leg out and used his foot as a final brake to stop the vehicle at the lights. The next day I reported the incident to the Police, but nothing further happened.

Chapter 9
Travellers and Local Passengers

Summer is a happy time for cab drivers. Not only are there hordes of U.K. residents who come to London to see the sights, but the school holidays add to the crowds. The number of Londoners 'Going on Family Holiday' doubles during those months. Railway stations, coach and air terminals full of travellers become a sure source of work. Luggage too, works in our favour, as it is so much easier to pop it into a cab, rather than drag it along a platform or stand it on an escalator to reach the underground train. Without a doubt some visitors become taxi passengers, and numbers mercifully rise throughout the summer months. During the same period the inward flow of foreign tourists also increases.

Late one night in central London my passenger, a Frenchman who spoke good English, queried the after-midnight surcharge of one shilling. Bighead that I am responded "Après midi, il est encore a shilling". Just one slight problem 'midi' should have been 'minuit'. After a silent mile, all became clear and we shared a good laugh.

Another language hiccup happened when a policeman stepped into the road and stopped me while I was searching for work near Liverpool Street. He was having trouble with his Italian, and could not understand what a passer-by was saying to him. Between the three of us it became clear that he wanted to get to NAPLES by air (not cab) as soon as possible. It appeared that either his coach had left the terminal or that he had a flight timed at 16:30. I did the best I could by driving him to the nearest travel agency. It would have been possible for me to have decided to drive him to Heathrow, earning a fortune for the journey, but I opted for the honourable solution.

What I had not taken into account was the slow diligence of the travel agent to whom I had brought him. This meant that one hour after I had taken him into the Agency, the young crane operator arriving from Ipswich, was not able to leave the country until much later that evening. While listening to the conversation between them, I learned that because of his work isolated in a tower, way above the world he had little opportunity to mix with English speakers and learn the language. The previous evening, he had received a cable from home informing him a close relative was seriously ill and failing, and that he should return home post haste. Having received permission to leave work, he was informed by an Ipswich travel agent of a flight which left for home at 16:30. All we succeeded in doing in London was to put him on a flight which left later that night. I drove him to the BOAC terminal at Victoria and handed him to an Italian speaking hostess. After that debacle, I started and have since continued, to study Italian for the last two years. A little school Latin started me on my way.

Pakistani immigrants created a furore for the London cab trade, there were insinuations that we were exploiting the newcomers before they had a chance to competently cope with the fresh environment. In those years, groups of them were apparently being taxi driven to the far corners of the United Kingdom. Such journeys were undertaken without the understanding that the normal fare was and is a king's ransom. There was perhaps, a modicum of truth in the accusations but the fact was these immigrants arrived at Heathrow airport penniless and the only form of transport that does not demand payment in advance is of course the cab trade. The assumptions for this type of journey were, that on arrival at the far-flung destination someone there would pay the amount due. One day soon after the High Commissioner for Pakistan declared that cab drivers were behaving unscrupulously, I chanced to put on the BOAC town terminal. There was a coachload of Asian immigrants disembarking. One of the passengers spoke English and put a punter into my cab, giving me the address to which he should be delivered in the East End of London. Crossing from West to East London we arrived at the destination not so far from where my grandparents who came from Lithuania lived, and where my mother was born.

The street was desolate in the extreme, and many years later came to be part of Banglatown. There were bomb sites galore and tenement type accommodation. We found the precise address and went inside together. The building reeked of cooking odours and the last household decorations were clearly pre-war. I found myself bound up with the adventure of my handsome young passenger. He exhibited constant apprehension, his demeanour as we investigated the building was of wariness.

He had trusted me to take the correct fare from his outstretched palm. He was so young and thin that I did not believe he would have the strength to lift his luggage himself. It appeared to be bedding. Everything that he saw, seemed strange to him. We entered the hallway and together we climbed the stairs, neither of us daring to leave his bed roll bags behind. Halfway up I shouted for Mahomet Ali for this was the name which was written on the paper I had been given. We came across a six- or seven-year-old girl, who had come to see what the noise was about. I asked her if she knew Mahomet Ali and she told me that he had moved to Bradford a couple of weeks earlier. I knocked on the door of the room/flat where he had dwelt. No reply. Now I banged on the door, and someone answered it at last. No, he was not Mahomet Ali and did not recognise the young, new arrival, and goodbye. I pleaded with him to say something to the newcomer. He did so reluctantly, and slowly, a conversation started. I slipped away silently having given the newcomer his first contact in this strange part of the world.

Occasionally I am a silent observer to a small drama passive and impotent, unable to stop a train of events that are in motion, and I remain useless in the vehicle. On a dark autumn night such an incident happened when a Trinidadian hired me near the top of Ladbroke Grove and asked me for the Western Fever Hospital. He was carrying his 3-year-old son who was moaning pathetically. We arrived at the Hospital which is solely residential, and has no outpatients' department and the gate keeper asked for the boy's admission papers. He had none. His father said all he needed was medicine for his son's whooping cough. The helpful gate keeper said this was simply not possible, but he would phone through to the registrar and duty sister. He was however not given permission to let the pair through the gate. Subsequent discussion proved that the family GP had declared the child was not ill. He had already been to the local hospital, where the duty doctor had declared the youngster might have whooping cough, but treatment for this was not in his purlieu, and he suggested the father and son visit the Western Fever Hospital. Reluctantly I was obliged to drive the pair home with no solution, neither medicine, diagnosis, nor treatment. The sound of the child's pitiful moaning remained in my ears the rest of the night.

The other week I helped an American couple find the tour bus that they had left a couple of hours earlier, but could not remember where. I quizzed them until they gave me a clue as to where, and what could be seen when they left the coach stop. In a City of the size of London there is an infinite number of complicated events which can and do occur. Another evening, driving a happy young mother home from hospital with her brand-new baby, I realised why this work is never boring, and, is frequently rewarding.

Female passengers brighten my day. The manner in which they seat themselves shows their manners or not. There are various ways to sit down: a thump, as a body hits the seat, or nothing. But rarely am I obliged to turn to see if the rider is seated, and it is actually safe to drive. At the end of a journey there is sometimes a whiff of perfume as a woman prepares for a meeting. One scent was so perfect I asked for its name so I could buy it for my wife as a present.

I have driven a girl who was late and took a cab over the shortest feasible distance to give the impression to the man she was meeting, that she had travelled the entire journey by cab. I hope she succeeded to impress him.

The current fashion of super long strings of beads is awkward for the wearer because they catch onto everything such as door handles, and I fear one day they will trip the wearer up. Fashions can be treacherous. During 'Beehive Hairstyle' it was touch and go if the owner could get in and out of the cab without ruining an expensive coiffure.

Exiting a West End hotel dressed for a banquet, a lady in a tulle ballgown had the doorman open a double door to let the gown through, then it took two men, the doorman, and her partner, to squeeze it into the cab. The man was later to be squashed in the corner of the taxi. I really cannot remember if he stood the entire journey in order not to crush the gown.

There are times when I am contented having a job simply driving and getting paid for it; sometimes there is the bonus of watching people's relief when they stop my taxi. There should be an ode written on stopping one's first taxi. Some expressions are pure gratitude, as the wheels stop turning and the cab glides to a halt by their side. Finally, there is my relief when I know the required destination. Some punters simply have a train to catch or an appointment to keep. The look of pride when a young person hailed me for his parents is only paralleled when an elderly gentleman manages to successfully hail me, proving to his companions that he still knows a trick or two.

Those punters are unaware of the reciprocal relief a driver feels when he traps a fare, for without them, he might as well be sitting at home. These initial feelings slowly change en-route, and when the rider steps out of the cab a new dynamic is in play. There are occasional passengers that have an inherent distrust of cab drivers.

The initial geniality, verbal and visible relief exhibited at the start of the journey disappear, wariness, and sometimes disdain take their place. The punter is where he needs to be, there is time to spare. The oaf at the wheel requires payment and a tip. I find it hard to recall when a couple leave the cab, for both to wish me a simple, "Good Night".

Some believe that any deviation from the main road is a confidence trick. Soon after Mayfair's fashionable Bond Street became One Way a middle-aged man who expected me to stop when he raised his right eyebrow, was so shocked when I sailed past that he actually raised his right hand. Unaware that I was unable to return to pick him up, he approached me warily. I explained that Bond Street was now One Way and had been thus for several weeks, he did not bother to reply but made the sort of noise with his teeth that indicated distrust. I was next informed that he did not argue with taxi drivers, and that he had been in Bond Street only last week, and that all was well then. A few questions from me uncovered that he had been driven by a chauffeur and he had not paid any attention to the route. In a similar manner, I have been told by a fare who professed to be in a hurry, to remain in the traffic jam on Regent Street rather than travel quickly along the parallel Savile Row W 1., which I had suggested as an alternative route.

Over the years that I have been driving, I have become accustomed to the ploys of would be passengers. Initially I could not see that there was any reason to set a trap for a taxi driver, but there are members of the public who consider it necessary. Night time is a period when drivers must be on the watch – drunken passengers can be generous, or more likely bad when they either vomit or are prepared to fight me for the fare. If there is a crowd of merry young fellows who exit from a pub and have a problem finding their way home, it makes sense to send out the soberest to the curb, namely, the one who can stand upright.

A dark night saw me flying over Westminster Bridge, when I was brought to a halt by a couple of youths wearing leather jackets and jeans, when out of the darkness another four faces appeared. They had been looking out over the river Thames and because of their all-black clothing, were not visible when I stopped. The address they required gave cause for concern – they asked for Tower Bridge. Not a likely place for them to live. So, at 03:00 I drove fast alongside the Thames hoping there was not to be trouble at the end. I was not encouraged at the way they peered through the party window at me and continued to insist I drove faster. I had started to console myself with the thought of the policeman on duty at the Bridge, when I realised a few "Left here Johns" and a "Right there Jim" and I would be miles away from the law. But all ended well.

I cannot resist shuddering when I recall the charming fellow that managed to wriggle his shoulders onto the long passenger seat, and then started to attempt to kick out the party window between us. A few vicious swerves kept him from succeeding, and I changed direction deciding to drive into Hammersmith police station on Shepherds Bush Road. The nearest police station I could think of. The entrance was to their yard was not easily visible, so I stopped the cab and raced across the pavement to the front door of the police building, but my inebriated passenger was there waiting for me. Suddenly he became aware of where he was, and he scarpered. I calmed down and continued to work, promising myself to be more vigilant about who I picked up. In those naive days there were no remote door locks

There are those who know precisely what they are doing when they walk in opposite direction to the way they wish to travel, in order to stop a taxi. They want to travel outwards to the periphery of London late at night, and they know that plenty of cabs have been out there and want to get back into the centre where and while, there is still plenty of work. They are aware that drivers are not keen to return to the sticks where there is a dearth of jobs - doubly so, at night. I endeavour to prevent entry into the vehicle before they give the address. That was in the years before there were automatic door locks. The pavements are often empty of pedestrians at night, so if I keep my eyes skinned, I am able to spot people changing direction from a half mile away.

I had to laugh one Boxing Day when I was trying to finish at 04:00 and could barely keep my eyes open. I passed a young fellow walking in the direction I was travelling. I slowed for him, but he was not interested. I continued on my homeward path relishing the thought of a cup of tea and bed, when a couple of hundred yards further on, I saw a girl walking alone. I stopped when hailed, as she too, was travelling towards my suburb. Then a plan they had patented was acted on: as she held the cab door open the single pin I had just passed, ran up to enter the cab. I do not believe that they had had a row, I think that they had decided that a cab would perhaps not stop for a couple but would stop for a young lady. How devious can you get?

Homeward bound for supper, the only place where I can usually be sure of the direction of the rider is at a bus stop. Needless to say, that maxim did not work when I picked up a rider, who was unaware that he was standing on the wrong side of the road. Being full of hope I suggested he should cross the road when he was told of his mistake and stand at the correct bus stop opposite, I optimistically indicated the correct place to stand. However, he was not in the least interested in crossing the road and catching the correct bus. "Take me there driver". My supper that night was drier than it should have been.

Chapter 10
Cabs and Drivers

Every driver believes in luck. This is manifested in many ways. It is more than baby's boots swinging from the rear-view mirror. Some drivers believe that certain cabs are lucky (I have recently come to the conclusion that some cabs are *unlucky*). *The regular drivers* refuse to drive any cab other than the one usually given to them. Some will *not turn round on their luck*. If they are having a good day or night, and after they have set down, they will only drive *forwards* and not return the way they came, even if it means an extra mile or so. After work a nightman, on arriving at the garage and nattering with the all-night washer, will simply declare "I had a bad night", or "I could not do anything tonight". What he means is, how much he had taken and whether his tips were any good.

Leaving the garage to go to work the farewell of the staff is a simple "Be Lucky". When things are running and I am having a good evening, I can time and time again pick up in the darkest narrowest back street and continue my shift with nary a 'dead mile'. Other nights, I can drive through London's West End with my 'For Hire' light shining and alluring, but no one will see me. It is as if the six-foot high fifteen-foot-long vehicle has turned invisible; no one is interested.

The psychology of tips leaves me wondering, how did this custom arise? Why are they given? Why do they give so much? So little? Why nothing at all? Primarily, it must depend on the mood of the passenger, secondly on his personal finances, and lastly on the driver, and whether he has been affable or not. The nearest round figure to the actual fare is often the criterion by which the tip is given.

If I am having a 'bad' night, it might well start if I am poorly paid and when I see the total amount in my hand, I bite my tongue and do not say "That's not a bad tip, what about the fare?". More than once in my exasperation, I forgot to reset the clock, so I would be driving around losing money every few yards I drove onwards. In those days, I paid in, on the meter, and every yard driven with the clock down was costing me. Obviously and additionally, no one would hail me as my lights were off. With more money being clocked with each turn of the road wheels, the sum could quickly accumulate on top of the lousy tip I had just received. The evening then being rubbish, I would trap, only to find myself setting down in a remote part of London where no one uses cabs. The bad set down would find me on my way back into work. When the fates decreed a bad night, my next job would return me to the sticks. The pattern for the evening set, I would find myself driving more dead miles than full.

But to be frank, taxi driving suits me. The job gives me the chance to be my own boss. Compared to the criteria of normal jobs, I do not have to participate in office chitter chatter and the inevitable rivalries for promotion. I agree that the work is frequently lonely, but I really do have the opportunity to decide for myself that I am having a bad day, and can decide I will finish now. In the sort of situation described in the previous paragraph, I would simply say "enough", and return home. All of this makes taxi driving seem to be the ideal trade for independently minded men and women.

The cab owners are unperturbed if a regular driver comes in early, accepting that a reliable driver can work a short day and he the boss will not be out of pocket if the cab is standing against the wall for a couple of hours. It is not the end of the world.

Like many tradesmen, a cab driver is able to pick his clients, steering clear of gangs of youths and drunkards, and one can kid oneself who will and who will not be a good tipper. On the other hand, there is another relationship which the journeyman has, and that is with the owners. The drivers here, perhaps have an upper hand as they can complain about mechanical problems with the taxi. They can also dictate the hours they work, and it is up to the proprietors to match the hours that journeymen work, fitting and sorting day men with the long night men. Many of the garages from which I have worked employ a dispatcher who makes sure that the maximum use of the cabs in the fleet is attempted, while reconciling the times journey men are available to work.

As a journey man it is not easy to combine our family and social lives. Trying to meet someone during working hours is a problem, for within the half hour I could be five miles away. Taking into account traffic is moving at 10 mph, a rendezvous then demands ceasing to work about 40 minutes before the arranged time. A job in the wrong direction could be double the time to return, and a job in the correct direction, could make me far too early.

I started work with Levy's of York Way as it was then, as they were able to give me a cab to wangle with. With a large fleet they always had spare cab for this and that. I still have the first Christmas present I ever received from work. Levy's gave me a wonderful set of teatime crockery.

Later I changed garages to one nearer home, I became the 'odd jockey'. I was given any cab which was available, which sadly was a different cab every day, and as any driver knows, each vehicle has its own idiosyncrasies. Certain cabs have sharp brakes, or a loose clutch, some cabs have trafficators that do not return (remember the orange sticks which flapped upwards on the sides of the vehicle. Over the years these flaps grew into a pair of ears attached to the roof of the cab). There were cabs that juddered greatly, and being the 'odd jockey', the new man gets the lot. After a while the monotonous regularity of the problems become tedious, and I obviously could not report a new problem each night. The regular driver makes sure any defects to his cab are reported and repaired and feels comfortable at the wheel of his usual cab. In the end, a new driver turns into a regular and gets his own taxi, and when I had my regular cab, I was contented.

Over the years I had worked from various garages, Levy's in York Way Kings Cross WC1, Pierce's in Battersea Park Road SW11. That was followed by a garage in Goldhawk Road, Shepherd's Bush (they experimented for a while with gas propelled cabs, but the weight of the gas container coupled with safety concerns made it too expensive to continue with the experiment), then afterwards at Farm Lane SW6. close to Chelsea Football pitch. The last place I rented was Graham Road, Dalston E8. Owning my own cab brought me into contact with Mann and Overton, just off the Wandsworth Bridge Road. They were the suppliers and repairers in chief of Austin Cabs and later when I bought from them, I chose the latest model the FX4.

To this day, after many variations of design, the 35 feet turning lock still reigns. It facilitates the taxi changing direction in narrow streets in a single movement.

This 35-feet turning lock was actually forbidden during my driving years. When Earnest Marples was Minister for Transport, cabs were not permitted to make 'U' turns. This I believe was merely a flexing of muscles. However, he recanted, and again we can legally turn on the spot mostly with a minimum of traffic disruption.

Other new specifications included moving the hinges of passenger doors to the opposite side, so that if by mistake, the door opened in transit, the wind pressure would blow it closed. Today's taxis will not permit the doors to open as long as the road wheels are turning.

Later in my life, after an aunt had given me a loan to buy a cab, our lives changed completely. I was now the boss and was freer than ever to plan my working life. As an owner driver, I became a 'mush'. Not a mess or a vegetable, but an abbreviation of the word 'mushroom', which was the shape of the electric meter (clock) which measures the distance and time driven on taxi journeys.

Soon after becoming a mush, my wife and I having parked up the cab, strolled down Portobello Road on a sunny Saturday afternoon. We saw a beautiful garnet ring which we bought, and used up every penny we had on us. We had intended to go to the cinema that night, so I deposited my wife with some friends, who lived nearby off Ladbroke Grove, and went to work. I did a couple of jobs to make just enough to pay for the cinema tickets and nosh. Not everyone can do this, and times have changed. To be honest I have not pulled this stunt again.

Near the Portobello Market a distraught young woman in a smart blue suit wildly hailed me, and asked if I knew where she could buy an ivory toothpick. The neighbourhood where she stood prompted me to reply, "In an antique shop". She was not pleased at this suggestion as she had tried them all (she said), and none had a *SECOND HAND* toothpick for sale. I observed that toothpicks were rather personal. She was not put out and instructed me to drive to another group of shops in Kensington Church Street. She tripped gaily from one to the other until at last, she returned.

"Did you get one" I asked. "Yes, but it is new" in a disappointed tone. I blinked and we drove off.

A driver will work as many hours as he wants, depending on his personal overheads. Naturally, the traditional 'butter boy' will work long hours not believing his luck, and indeed, it is a fact that everything soon begins to fall into his lap. I remember coming back from abroad and driving for the first time in ages, and everyone I saw seemed to want a cab. This was simply because I was hyper acute, and as usual, my senses became less active with time. Repetition equals lack of awareness.

There are drivers who cannot stand the traffic, and prefer to work exclusively at night, hoping to avoid the hold ups in traffic. It is also a fact that after a serious night shift, I arrive home and find myself still quivering, even after half an hour indoors. Full concentration on driving safely, plus constantly searching for a raised hand did that to me. This could of course be allayed by sitting on a rank. But even there, I could begin to wonder why no one is leaving the hotel, or underground station, and needing a cab. One needs to be 'with it' to get the most out of the job.

During a much-needed holiday, I dreamed that I was driving a tandem bicycle and that the fare was in a hurry to get to the station. No doubt a psychologist would have a dozen reasons for the dream, but a successful driver always needs to concentrate, and the intensity does not die away instantly. Night work poses the question of sleeping during the day hours, so most drivers work day shifts to avoid that complication. If one is sufficiently established in life, all one needs, is to earn enough for a glass of beer or two. In my retired years, having paid for most of our possessions, and having accumulated a little capital, I was able to supplement our small income by working for a month per year. 28 days, with no days off, made the most of the rental fee. With this booster we were able to demurely exist.

Early on when I was working on a night shift, I wrote up the following trauma:

"Four pillows and two cotton wool ear plugs were insufficient to keep out the noise of happy size ten boots tramping the bare floorboards in the flat above my head. The cotton wool seems to make my ears tingle

(I guess that is why there are now wax earplugs), and just as teeth are set on edge by a noise, so was my sleep deprived, being woken with each step over my head. Two pillows above and two under my head hardly diminished the thumping created above my head by the jubilant moving men.

My bedroom competed with Bank Underground Station, for as fast as one trolley was loaded with books from our overhead neighbour's extraordinary library, the next was on the move down the corridor of bare floorboards. The usual noises in the block had been the result of the redevelopment of decent sized accommodation, being modified to that of a rabbit hutch. Investors needing good returns, created apartments for pigmies. The luxury flats created for the old-fashioned Victorian era were an obvious easy target for them.

In our previous mansion block, where we lived, they utilised a team of workmen who had a foreman called JEDD. JEDD the mighty, JEDD the superb, JEDD the indefatigable who was apparently indispensable, so for months at a time "Oi JEDD" reverberated around all the communal areas, penetrating every nook and cranny in every room, including my bedroom and finally through the two feather pillows covering my head. My being was saturated with *SUPERMAN JEDD*. I could visualise him tearing out a fireplace with one hand while scanning a wall out of the corner of his eye, and hitting the focal point with his elbow, and down the wall would crumble, leaving a hole, waiting for the door which JEDD would flick into place with a nonchalant gesture.

Yesterday haunted by Jedd from my old home, and associating myself with him, I was tempted to leap out of my bed and tell the size ten boots, all six or eight of them, what I thought of them. Suddenly it occurred to me that they might not see me as the manly figure I considered myself. For certainly, I would look ridiculous in my dressing gown with the sweater covering my pyjamas to help fight a hypochondrial fever, plus a silk scarf tied round my neck to relax some twisted neck muscles; and all this at 11:00. No, I had better lie still and work out what I would write, and so calm myself.

Shortly after this, I became tempted to consider going on day work even if it meant my losing some income.

As a Licensed driver one can ply for hire wherever one pleases so long as it is inside Metropolitan London, we are not confined to any area. Some areas act as magnets: City, Railway Stations, Mayfair, Chelsea, Oxford Street, Aldgate, Whitechapel, Air Terminals, and drivers are attracted to them. The only item that the driver must have, is a 'Green Badge'.

There are those who work from the 'Green' (Camberwell) or the 'Junction' (Clapham). Some like Golders Green Station, others favour 'Archway'. There are in these places a steady flow of passengers even if the work tends to be local. Cabmen who do not 'work' these ranks could be ostracised by the regulars, when they 'put on'. Albeit there is much more time on these ranks to read the papers and smoke a pipe, while watching local activities and life in general.

It was a warm autumn day when I sat there on Haverstock Hill NW3 not too far from the Royal Free Hospital. I read the LTDA taxi magazine/newspaper, which not only records cabmen's take on life but also records a slant on society in general. The issue in my hand contained comment on the advent of minicabs, and the new British vogue of mini this and mini that. A rise in the cost of fuel which would later be reflected in the cost of living, an assault and robbery of a driver and at last a new model taxi – the FX4. A story from a cab man in Australia, and a comparison of taxis in Old World Paris, and the New World San Francisco. A letter from a nearly retired driver of about how things used to be, complaints of how the fogs, or more recently smogs, made work nigh on impossible. The story of a drunk fare and a belligerent fare, a query of the wording of a petition, and to round it all off, stories of racial antagonism to a Jew and a Black man. This issue of the magazine seemed to me, to be a perfect example of how drivers are involved in every facet of metropolitan and world life.

I finally understood the significance of the absence of the central driving mirror when on a Friday night a couple entered the taxi, close to Trafalgar Square. It was the lady who asked to be driven round the park. OK. I concede I am naïve, but the request was a trifle strange as it was dark, and I could not imagine what there was to be seen. I enquired which park, and received a sharp retort from the young woman, who seemed to be in charge of the pair. It was only when I found my way into St. James Park, did I realise what was going on behind me, and I tried to keep the cab on an even keel. I was instructed to drive more slowly, and stupidly asked where should I go next? Yes, it was the young man, who when the journey ended, paid me off. I think his name must have been John (sometimes known as 'The John'), and they left the vehicle as they had found it. We had returned to Trafalgar Square.

The New York City fathers decided that the FX4 and the earlier FX3 were immoral vehicles, and would not licence the vehicle since the passengers' knees rubbed against one another, if it was a full house. Over the years the discussion continued and then the reckoning was, that 4 in a cab was not a danger to propriety. If only the London Authorities would become as modern. It took years before central driver's mirror was authorised. The precise details of a cab's structure have to be approved by the relevant Home Office department before a new design is passed.

In later years when disabled persons became more recognised, a ramp was designed so that a wheelchair could roll into the cab. The facility is so much of a drag for the taxi driver that it is used only in extremis. Another development on behalf of the disabled person is a step which allegedly appears between the pavement and cab floor. Today in 21st C. the jump seat nearest to the curb, swivels making it nearly possible for a disabled person to sit down in a single inward movement. Item by item there is a debate. The new FX4 has four doors, unlike the FX3 which was aptly named *a side loader* because of where the luggage went. Now instead of straps, there is a door to keep the luggage safe.

Agreed, four doors: but where is the running board. How do the disabled enter if there is no extra step? But even when an elderly person enters, their spine is hurtfully bent, or otherwise their heads would remain outside the taxi. Computers have made their way into the clock, and the tariff runs at three different speeds, taking into account the weekend, the late and later hours of a day.

At work, it takes an acrobatic movement for me to manually open the brand-new curb side window, to ask for the destination and later to receive payment when the passenger is back on his feet on the pavement. I have tried it all: leave the curb side window open and preserve my sacroiliac (or slip a disc), alternatively leaving the driver's side window closed. With both windows open there is an icy tornado circling me. 21st

Century design with the concomitant costs, allow the driver to not budge, as the window opens at the touch of a button. The little aperture now evident in the glass partition though designed for the passenger to pay the driver is not often used. Personally, as a passenger, I am too scared to use the credit card device stuck on the interior of the cab nowadays in 2022.

In those primitive days there was no heating either for drivers or passengers. I just wish there had been a happy medium. In 1960s some warmth from the engine was allowed to flow into a heating system. The work of a seated driver leaves him more or less motionless for the entire shift. It was so cold, that any movement provided some warmth, even having to contort myself towards the passenger.

The breaks to find a public toilet which was safe, and the brief stops for snacks provided the sole physical movement during the working day. Sitting driving cannot be described as movement. I agree we move our limbs but in a most limited manner. In my nightmares I slowly turn into a fixture of the cab, and meld into it becoming a part of the bodywork, being aware of directions, streets and 'points'. I Howard am no longer required, I am metamorphosed into a driverless vehicle that knows it all, drives safely and sit in the front seat as a mere spectator or owner.

The driver's immobility is unhealthy, and an acquaintance of mine grew such a large corporation, that he had to have a square of leather stitched to his outer garment to prevent the constant rubbing of the steering wheel from wearing out his clothes. That was before there were satellites flying round the world with a direct connection to moving vehicles instructing drivers where to turn and park. I believe they call it GPS. Occasionally, nowadays, I have the pleasure of hearing my mobile phone giving the wrong directions while I am driving in my own car. Silently I smile to myself, thankful that I have the Knowledge.

Yes, in my day we still had the words 'FOR HIRE' shining brightly from our foresail. The difficulty to create the word 'TAXI' was still a dream of the future. So, we sailed the streets disguised as 'For Hire' until someone managed to change the plastic sign.

Some six months after I had started work, I met a friend who commented on seeing me, "You have lost weight". I understood immediately that I had put on weight and was being told so. From then onwards I decided to watch my diet, for I am always tempted when having a cup of tea to add the odd bun or cake. During discussions later in life, I discovered that it is possible to order a cup of tea and not add any additional items to the order. There was not, and is not, a tradition of noblesse oblige in workman's cafes.

Bernard Levin writing in the Daily Mail of his adventures, when riding in the new FX4 taxicab, kept me amused for days and I had to restrain myself from laughing at my punters, for he wrote: "I had to go down on my knees to address the driver from the passenger compartment". He then complained of the tiny little window in the centre of the glass partition was super complicated to open. To round the piece off, he described his struggles to physically exit the cab.

He, Levin, who later wrote for the Times Newspaper, pulled on chrome bracket after bracket (I presume one or two of them were handles to aid passenger stability), then he emptied an ashtray or two, the contents sliding into his trousers' turn ups. All this before he succeeded in opening the door to leave the cab. His final and justifiable complaint was the difficulty he had in paying through the two-inch slit in the curb-side window, which the driver had left open just enough to keep the cold out.

Recently (in 2023) as a passenger, I have made the mistake of speaking to my wife while the intercom microphone was open. The driver listened and wisely did not interject his opinions. Personally, in this century I do not ride often enough to be able to find out how to put a Credit Card into the paying device which many taxis seem to have.

Shepherd's Bush Rank

Chapter 11
Radio, Traffic Flow and Tips

My method of working the cab tends to change if there is a two-way radio installed. Reflexively, I tend to point the cab to the areas where the jobs are being called. Unfortunately, as with all taxi work, it is never where my cab is! When I am located where jobs are, I have a choice: to remain or leave the area. In either case my normal routine has been interrupted, for I usually point the cab to neighbourhoods where there are concentrations of pedestrians needing cabs.

The employers claim that the radio does not give them extra income, and some are loathe to pay for its costs. They maintain they only put radio into the cab to keep the drivers happy. But there is a school of drivers who even when they are given a radio cab will not use it. The drivers say it distracts them from usual methods of working. There is a scheme afoot for every cab to have a radio, and thus provide all London coverage on an unprecedented scale. If the public were to dial TAXICAB, they would receive the taxi nearest to the caller. If this scheme comes to fruition, it will provide superb coverage. The downside might be that we would lose the connection with the man on the curb edge, who would have to find a phone before he got to the street. Availability on the streets is our greatest asset.

True or not, one night at Charing Cross Station, I joined the line of cabs as 'they were running' and found myself in a situation when I had one moment to solve a delicate situation involving public relations. The first three people in the queue were all more than drunk. If I pulled out of the station, there would be some 20 irritated taxi riders left waiting. If I picked up the trio, I had a potential problem (belligerence – your' taking the wrong route - no tip, - vomit). The latter would put me out of action for the whole night until the cab had been washed out. I took the coward's solution and pulled away.

Funny things are to be heard on the radio – "Albert is bursting" This simply means that the Albert Hall in Kensington is letting loose a mass of potential riders. The message "The Westminster Gas Works is on the burst" is self-explanatory.

On answering a radio call, finding the house number can be a problem. This is not unique to us. Postmen and delivery drivers have the same predicament. There were and still are the traditional odd and even house numbers system, then there are the consecutive numbers. There is a rough rule of thumb suggesting that house numbers begin at the end of the street nearest to St. Paul's Cathedral. However out in the sticks, it becomes difficult to guess where the cathedral is.

Earls Court has a diabolical numbering system, in some places the numbers rotate around the perimeter of a block. And then in Bayswater there are gardens which are faced with two different squares names on facing sides of the same green. Queens Square, Cleveland Square, and Cleveland Gardens.

In Belgrave Road SW1 there are three houses with the number 78. There is 78 Warwick Square, 78 Eccleston Square, and 78 Belgrave Road. A little confusing for the uninitiated, but all in a day's work for the London Cabby. I understand that Tokyo houses are numbered according to the order they are constructed!!
There is a legend suggesting that an East London street changes its name with each new premier.

Daily Demands for Taxis

Two or three times each day there is a shortage of taxis. The first is morning, as everyone turns up to work in Central London, so the majority of cabs drive inwards, some towards the City and some to the West End. There is a general bemoaning that there are never enough cabs.

Now there are masses of cabs milling round the centre of the Metropolis. A few drivers will point their cabs away from heart of the City, outwards, to catch the next wave of office and store workers as they make their way inwards.

Next is the time to hit the termini, the railway stations, airlines town terminals, and bus stations. As the morning rush hour diminishes so does the need for cabs, and there are more than enough taxis in every corner. Drivers start patrolling the roads looking for punters. There is a small increase of trade around the lunch hour, as extra persons come into

London and the workers rush to complete dinner dates and other central London activities. Personally, I have never noticed this, but the real rush hour is the evening, after work around 17:00.

The traffic and taxi flow has now turned around – mainly outwards bound. The actual problem is doubled by the changeover of day and night drivers. This coincidence of shifts complicates the situation.

I found when visiting Paris, that a driver returning home from work would carry a notice, stating that he was returning home, and to which arrondissement. If a potential passenger wishes to use the cab, he may do so. In London, there is no such arrangement, leaving many homeward bound taxis empty at that crucial time.

There is another minor rush on cabs as theatre goers arrive, either to eat prior to the performance or to have a drink in the theatre bar. The demand and supply balances itself out around 'closing time', when with a bit of luck, the longer distance jobs arrive. Pubs and theatres closing around 22:30, create the last wave of demand for cabs, at an advantageous time for drivers. The meter is now reflecting the late hour and runs faster.

But amongst the imponderables are the fares who jump into the cab when there is a shower, or it is a rainy day. They don't want to get wet, but I suspect, harbour an antipathy to the driver for charging so much more than the bus fare. The person I would expect to tip well would be a person in a hurry who tells me he has a train to catch. But for some reason, these persons do not tip well. Perhaps they do not have the time to tip, or maybe they are not regular cab riders, and are unaware of how poorly we are recompensed for our efforts. It would be a mistake to drive wildly in order that they might catch a train.

It happens that punters could climb into the cab in a generous mood, and do not wait for the change to be given. If the driver is surly and aggressive, he might receive a larger tip in order to preclude a situation, but that strategy might ricochet. No matter how many pounds worth of coins one carries they can run out, and four consecutive pound notes can empty the kitty. This, justly or unjustly, does upset some passengers when the driver cannot furbish the correct change.

A lesson I learned early in life happened when I was travelling with a pair of rather heavy trunks. I had a porter at Victoria Station help me to the train, and he hoisted the trunks into the carriage. Unfortunately, I did not give a large enough tip and he left me and walked away without a word, only to reappear at the far end of the carriage and shout down the length of the Pullman Carriage what he thought of me. Lesson learned. On arrival in Brighton Station, I probably massively over-tipped the porter there.

The ways of porters vary from station to station. At some mainline stations the door is opened by a willing porter who is not disappointed if there is no luggage. At others one has to whistle, beckon or cajole the porter to approach the cab. I have noticed that at one station there is a roster system as on a cab rank, and porters take their turn as it comes up. There is an equal esprit de corps as with cabs, and on one occasion, luggage which was handled by a single porter to load, needed a pair of men to unload it. One man efficiently arranged the baggage at Liverpool Street Station, yet by the time we had arrived at Victoria it must have doubled in size, for the porter who eventually responded to our calls walked all round my cab not believing his eyes.

The punter and I both had bother controlling our laughter until the porter spoke, "Want to come in with me on this one Bert?". Bert sauntered over, and they began to unload the cab and I could return to work.

At the end of a run, the punter might say to me "Give me a bob" (a shilling) concealing in his hand the money he is about to pay with; I am fairly sure that he is about to give me a tip of which he or she is ashamed, and will depart as soon as possible. Another gimmick of the 'generous' is to pay with what appears to the novice as three half-crowns, is in fact a half-crown covering two florins (two shilling pieces).

On the other hand, I watched the man who entered the cab, give the doorman of his Mayfair club a £1 note. He must have seen my eyes bulging, for he told me "Don't worry – nothing like that for you!". But there was, and I was simultaneously astounded and delighted. There is I believe, a continental standard whereby the shorter the journey the larger the tip. I believe I enjoyed the benefit of the mixture of these two customs.

There are drivers who believe that the best part of their income is the manner in which they can 'chat up' a punter, and these drivers will not take out a cab which has a noisy engine, or an FX4 as talking through the glass is difficult. Our garage in Battersea has a driver who I believe is a competitor with Baron Munchhausen, for the most extraordinary things that happen to him, or so he says. Upon consideration, it seems to be an idiosyncrasy of every other driver I speak to. These drivers are always getting jobs to the airport (the very best a driver could wish for) and are frequently being invited home by their riders. For myself, nothing so exotic happens, except perhaps when once, carelessly, my fare took out her money and absent mindedly handed me her house keys in lieu of the fare.

There are days when I feel like a road hog, there are days when I drive in a considerate manner. Deep in my psyche there is imbedded a feeling, that driving the public I have special road rights, and the more so, because of my expertise in road craft. I definitely did not start my career feeling like this, but the minicab drivers adopted it within minutes of starting work. Gradually, and I believe justly, I have developed the opinion that cab drivers are more aware of the overall road situation where they are driving, and know more precisely than most, what can and cannot be done with their vehicles. The 1962 Road traffic Act makes no provision for professional drivers, for it declares that everyone who errs is equally culpable if they break the law.

On my first job one morning, a young person hailed me and indicated the direction I was to drive. It was straight through three lanes of stationary traffic on the other side of the road. Still fresh from my Christmas break, I smiled rather than snarled, and though the traffic was only moving in fits and starts, it took much belligerence to penetrate the three lanes at right angles. Everyone seemed unable to see me pushing through, even though the cab was painted black. Job done. I asked my fare if she knew what was causing the hold up. She replied "No", and went into the ritual condemnation of the Knightsbridge underpass. I knew then that I was back at work, and repeated my usual reply: "It took three years to build and it only takes 30 seconds to drive through it". The jams were the same as when I had started my winter break. I assumed that the people sitting in the jam were not the same ones as before Christmas. Suddenly, I became magnanimous and did not cross when the lights were green in my favour, thus not blocking the cross traffic as I could not clear the junction. This obviously pleased the cars waiting to cross, but the vehicles behind me became infuriated and hooted to high heaven.

We arrived at the destination, and then I heard the ominous words "Wait a moment will you driver?". I waited five minutes and then she pranced prettily towards me, forgetting that the meter had been running all the time she was absent. A maidenly smile was the compensation in place of the extra fare which had clocked up.

Next job:" "Air Terminal please, and I have been waiting here fifteen minutes".

Now a plea, "Get us to Holborn Town Hall quick-ish, someone is caught in a lift and is starting to become panicky". Not possessing the alarm bell the emergency services have, I dared not break any traffic laws. Fate was against the trapped person, as each signal turned red as we approached it. At long last we arrived, however during the journey time, I had not learned how to repair the lift fault, but I did know what had gone wrong, and what should be done to rectify it. I also learned the quickest manner to contact the repair team, should I ever need to do so.

It was a good day, and the jobs appeared regularly, until by chance I passed the precise spot where, only a couple of hours ago, I had trapped for the Air Terminal. The taxis were passing, empty, one every minute, exactly where my fare had stood and waited 15 minutes in desperation. Such are the vicissitudes of finding a cab. None, or too many. The rush hour had faded into the daily monotony of tedium. It was now time to drive in circles at an ever-decreasing speed.

Before I returned to Pearce's garage, I totted up the day's takings, deducted the 2 mock 2/6ps, added 25 US cents, and put aside the 25 Malaya and British Borneo Ringits for my foreign coin collection. The worry of when I would be able to spend this money was balanced by the thought of the friendly fare who waved me goodnight from outside his Chelsea home.

On other occasions, even during a short job, my mind runs through a wide gamut of thoughts. *At last, someone has hailed me, I am really glad, I was having one of my invisible evenings...... One tonne of machinery and no one can see me. Don't know if I should have overtaken the last empty cab, half a mile ago, but he was only doing 20 and I can't seem to keep this cab under 30........ Forgot my ethics. Good, a nice tip, well it is Saturday night...... Think I will put on the rank in the station, only single file tonight as the newspaper delivery vans are unloading Sunday's papers to be shipped round the country.... Time to scribble a few notes. Move up the rank a bit, write a few more lines, move up. Write....move....*

"What's that Madam, Euston?"

The following day, sitting alone steeped in a special melancholy which this Lancaster Gate rank seemed to stimulate in me, I let myself daydream. The cab rank telephone remained ominously silent. There were no walk-up jobs during those moments, and there was quiet on the road. I thought of yesterday, and recalled days gone by. The rain gently soaked into the grass verges and yielded its special after rain drying scent. It melded with the elemental ceaseless patter on the hollow drum skin of the roof and bonnet; the combination of sound and smell created a sleepy timelessness. I daydreamed.

Was it only yesterday in Fenchurch Street Station that the lad approached me and asked me "How much to Gravesend?". He did not want Gravesend, but actually Southend. Bells began to ring in my head. He had, he said, been attacked by a dozen youths and they had taken his money. There was indeed a red bump on his forehead, and he may well have been speaking imperfect English, perhaps because of a wound to his mouth. There was an inconclusiveness about his story that diverted much of my sympathy – the police would not help with funds, neither would the railway authorities allow him to travel with a voucher. Racking my memory, I suggested that it might be possible for him to travel by bus, if he provided his name and address and paid later.

He walked off in the direction of the Aldgate Bus Terminal, and I wondered how it must feel to be an alien in Britain – or for that matter an alien anywhere. The boy had a strong European accent.
Now, I remembered as I sat there with the rain still beating its message on the vehicle body, the pair of demobbed soldiers who said they had just come from East Africa. This event had happened to me a couple of years ago. Nevertheless, the incident was still clear in my mind. I

visualised the manner in which they jeered at every African looking passer-by as we drove to Kings Cross Station. Luckily the pedestrians did not know what was happening, for we were driving at road speed and whipped past them, they were unaware of the taunts.

This is the 1960s, but it was only last night in Kentish Town, when I drove alongside a van full of youthful yobs gesticulating and jeering. Passing them, I noted they were shouting and raving at a brown skinned family who were walking along the street. Mother father and three kids. Scarcely an adversary worthy of five youths. I could well imagine, the pangs of the parents and the bewilderment of the children. Sadly, there is no medicine to sooth the soul. There is no panacea. Early Race Legislation then, did, not tackle this type of crime. Even so, it needs time, plus the positive resolution of members of parliament to pass an act which might hinder this kind of racial taunting to have an effect on society. Witnesses are needed, a court room, documents, investigation, time in preparation, the presentation, a magistrate and finally administration of the penalty/fine.

Still, I had not 'got off' the rank. I recalled last week when I was having my cab repaired and lunch time arrived. The garage was in North London and half of the fitters were black, the remainder white. A West Indian mechanic had taken a guitar and had begun to strum the strings, when a white mechanic suddenly stood up and began gibbering like a gorilla jumping up and down on the spot, and waving his arms. Everyone laughed – it was the only thing to do. Yet, how many of the fitters seeing this happen bottled up bitterness, ready to explode sometime in the future.

These episodes did not just float up into my mind randomly, they were related to an incident in which I was involved only yesterday. I saw a Bakery van which was driven by a black driver. The door of the bread compartment was open and was swinging wildly as the van progressed. He had just overtaken me when I noticed the open door. I hooted at the driver to indicate that something was amiss and pointed at the door. This, it seems, was the last straw to him, in a series of well-intentioned signals. Each one being misinterpreted as a racial insult. The driver's rage increasing as the number of hoots on the horn grew. I indicated the van door once again and drove away. I had tried to help but had only made matters worse.

While sitting pondering the inequalities of life, I looked out of my side window and noticed a man, probably an American Serviceman, for we were in Lancaster Gate, home of the PX for US serving troops. He was smartly attired in a tea shirt, with a close cropped army haircut. It alarmed me every bit as much, when he began to pound the air around him looking at a rapidly departing car, and I feared that he too had been the recipient of taunts by passing yahoos. Out of reach of his massive fists, they sped away leaving him to nurture his malice until it dissipated. I observed this incident sitting safely on the Lancaster Gate rank. The road came back into focus as I jumped out to answer the obstinately silent until now, rank telephone. I was returned to my secure world of addresses and streets.

That same week driving to work on a Saturday afternoon, I entered my nth suburb of London's Metropolitan conurbation. Not too different from the previous one. Driving onwards towards the centre of town aiming at Bethnal Green Road, I succeeded in envisioning London as not just the capital of the UK, but as a throbbing heart, pumping trade, commerce, arts, tourists, and visitors, through its varied chambers. Each borough, a unit, which when added to the others, makes London, what it is, *The Centre of The World*. Financial activity, residential mazes, commercial factories, and sports centres, all vying to complete a plaid unique in the British Isles. Its pulse beats mightily, in order to serve the variety of its entirety. In Borough after Borough, running parallel to the river Thames, there are a sequence of venues, which have a life, character, and vitality of their own, each contributing to the capital city. Docklands, East End, City of London, West End, and onwards to football stadia, tennis venues, and rugby grounds. So much bustling activity is nestled inside its perimeter of suburban homes.

The arteries of the heart of London are the main roads leading lingeringly towards the centre to and through, the outer boroughs. They simultaneously lead away to the green swathes of fields known as the 'The Green Belt', that exists as a protection against an expanding city. The routes, allow the flow of persons and commodities inwards and outwards, unconsciously joining suburban district to suburban district. The roads are London's blood stream. It is sometimes said that London is an entity in its own right. To me, sitting at the steering wheel of a

Metropolitan cab, it is an honour to serve the giant, by transporting miniscule units from A to B inside this body.

That warm sunny Saturday afternoon showed me the sameness of High Street after High Street. The people might have been different, namely by incomes, ethnicities, education, and aspirations. There might be a slight difference in architectural style, depending on the decade in which the neighbourhoods were developed, but the set up was identical. Main road becoming the High Road and in turn The Shopping Street. Multiple stores jostling for trade, attracting customers to bustle up and down searching for bargains. The overcrowding creating a fervour, helping to empty purses and wallets filled with the week's wages. I contended with numerous buses which lumbered backwards and forwards moving the masses to and fro. I drove on. A new High Road, an identical set of premises binding together the sinews of the Capital's population.

A prosperous suburb has cinema, bingo hall, ice rink or dance hall. These differences being the single source of variety between districts. These centres of entertainment are a coy imitation of the more sophisticated West End.

Leaving the periphery and re-entering London that afternoon, my overall vision faded, as I concentrated harder on the individuals standing on the curb side and finding myself work. I was in truth, the same as everyone else bustling that Saturday afternoon, simply trying to sustain a family with clothes, a home, and placing food on the table.

Chapter 12
Personal Relations & My Longest Journey

The name 'Black Cabs' somehow associates itself with darkness and night, but it is the colour which dominated the exterior of the vehicle for many years. It was simply a measure of finance. Any other colour was more expensive. A vehicle with a bright colour was probably not a licenced taxi so no one would hail it. As early as 1853, Max Schlesinger writing about 'Sauntering in and about London' has little good to comment on Hackney Carriages and the drivers thereof. Henry Mayhew a decade later, has equally few kind words. He a co-founder of 'Punch' magazine, worried about the poverty stricken of London, and wrote a near encyclopaedia about London's destitute. A sad situation printed and ignored. Both writers even as far back as the nineteenth century had little good to report on the drivers of the then taxis.

The adage *"An empty taxi is in everyone's way, and everyone is in an occupied taxi's way"* is still worthy.

Akin to the way I felt when cross examined in a social setting, was similar to the manner we were virtually ostracised in the 'posh' block where we lived. It first annoyed us and eventually amused us. Part of the natural instinct of London and perhaps city society, is not to talk to your new neighbours for a year or so. However, this continued beyond that period. But the neighbourhood suited us, and this was where we wanted to live. Herbert Hodge, a taxi driver writing in the 1940s had similar trouble. He recalled that the trade of taxi driving was considered to be of a dubious nature, and he found great difficulty in acquiring accommodation. When at last he found a flat, he was allowed to live there on condition that he did not park his cab at the front door.

The attitudes of the Public and the Police are ongoing in this respect. Their assumptions about cab drivers have not changed in the last quarter century. One day my wife and I had to speak to a medical consultant. I recognise it is inherent that he talks down to anyone who is not a private patient, believing that if one used the NHS, he is probably uneducated and frequently, poor. But when he started talking to us and then discovered that I was a Cabby the downward angle increased. Perhaps a few words of mine might have thrown him off balance for a moment. Then he continued in the same vein. He spasmodically interjected into his words the patronising sentences "I can see that you are an intelligent sort of chap", and then proceeded to tell us what we both suspected, dubious information. He gave no help, advice or encouragement, for he was addressing one of an inferior group. The subject was more than serious – this was the period of Thalidomide.

Recently I was called to the Old Bailey as a Juryman. I found the experience harrowing if not onerous. The only part I enjoyed were the regular hours, and the way I could wear my best clothes, and carry an umbrella just like any other city gent. I started at 10:00 and had a reasonable break for lunch, and finished at 16:00 or 17:00. The case in question was a road accident, and the debate was over the responsibility for it. The plea if I remember correctly, was whether the driver of the vehicle was responsible, or whether the vehicle had been incorrectly maintained. To press home a point of discussion with the rest of the jury, as the case concerned a traffic incident, I told them that I was a cabby. I did this to illustrate for them that if my employer tells me to take out a particular cab, I do not give it a road test but assume that it is in good condition. Well knowing that some 5 minutes earlier, the previous driver will have finished his shift and if necessary, would have put in a complaint if something serious was amiss.

I have not the time or need to do a road test every day as I must assume the vehicle is roadworthy. This is surely not negligent of me. I made my point, though it seems to me that any jury of drivers will have difficulty in finding another driver guilty of negligence. In each person's mind there is the thought "there but for the grace of God go I". As it happens, every other person on the jury had a story to tell of a narrow escape while driving. I have long forgotten the details, but we found the accused 'Not guilty' of the driving offence.

It would not be an understatement that taxi drivers and even bus conductors need to do a course in public relations.

Joe Bloggs, sometimes known as John Smith, even without that important pint, owns an aggressive gene. It is latent until it starts to rain, or someone misses a football penalty, or the food was undercooked, then watch out. Taxi drivers deal with the most difficult type of person, some of whom are quite important in their own spheres. A typical problem occurred one night when I was patrolling the length of Jermyn Street SW1, when what appeared to be a sober gent hailed me outside one of the night spots. I stopped, and a client of the club was respectfully put into the cab, and everyone assured me, he was 'alright'. This means a multitude of things. In this case it meant he was drunk all right, the other connotations of alright were irrelevant. However, before I left this particular club the manager gave me half a crown for my kindness in stopping. This probably meant "you're in for trouble I am glad it is you and not me". Before I pulled away it was ascertained that the gentleman wanted to go to The Embassy, the nightspot not a diplomatic one. When we arrived at The Embassy, the manager and doorman were reverent in their insistence the gentleman could not enter, and once again assured me, he was 'alright'. They explained he was a city magnate (Magnum?) in Sherry. I did not believe them. However, they gave me his home address which they insisted was correct. We progressed to the road, my passenger slept, when he was not repeating the fashionable phrase "Quite, quite".

This phrase was quoted perhaps some hundred times. Arriving at the address, I rang the bell and knocked at the door, no response. Since one of the bedroom windows were open, I was sure someone was at home. The passenger was not only out cold, but he was so heavy he was practically impossible to move. I returned to the house and knocked again, to no avail. Once more, I returned to my cab to see if I had the correct address. Then I had no alternative but to see if 'Quite, quite' was carrying identification. I found a few documents which confirmed his name, so I had to assume the address was correct. I waited, looking for a policeman. Suddenly, a taxi appeared and set down; with a witness present I was able to search more thoroughly through his pockets until I found his house key. Then we two cab drivers went to the door that I had not succeeded in kicking down.

At the slightest rattle of the keys, 'Quite quite' became communicative, and while we had him awake, we found out the *true number of his house*. His lightning recovery allowed us to deposit him in his own doorway, and I went away much relieved though I had wasted a great deal of time and earned little enough money.

"Primrose Hill, Cock" "The Cally, John" (i.e., The Caledonian road) are just a few of the ways people address me. I wonder what would happen if I used the same terms of address that they use for me. Most amusing are the Kensington and Chelsea Toffs, who wish to show that they are among the cognoscenti who refer to me as 'Maite' in their usual nasal inflection, or there are still others who patronisingly address me as 'Govenaw'. They are trying to say 'Guv'.

I suppose I am a bit of a soft touch, but when a man comes up to me almost in tears and tells me that his wife has run away and that an aunt has to be called from the other side of London to look after the children, I fall for it. Then he continues that he has no money but that he will send it to me. Now I have to weigh up the situation, the man's urgent need against my financial loss, as I have to pay in 5/8ths of the takings registered on the clock. The fare was not paid, but on this occasion, a social obligation had been fulfilled.

Once or twice, someone has jumped in and said to me "Watch your step!" and continued "I am a lawman" in the same friendly manner. I have asked to see his identity card at the end of the ride. All I have ever read was 'Metropolitan...', the following words unfortunately obscured by a large thumb. I presume the persons involved were probably from the Metropolitan Water Board.

About 22:00 one night at Oxford Circus, a couple of young men jumped in and asked me to hurry after a cab which was fast disappearing down Oxford Street W1. I asked to see their Police passes and once again read METROPOLITAN THUMB. I actually jumped a few lights and nearly hit a few cars, and then suddenly realised my boss would not thank me if I dented a panel or two of his taxi. However, once clear of Oxford Street and Marble Arch we caught up with the taxi we were following and drove after it into the Ladbroke Grove W10 area. The other cab stopped, and I was about to pull up behind it, when they asked me to continue and then stop. It was only then I realised that they had probably done this kind of thing before, even if they only worked for the Metropolitan thumb.

Some women though, like to play it tough. No tulle or fancy dress for them, merely dark glasses and raincoat, plus long tall dark bespectacled friends. One such couple requested Kentish Town, and then in the manner of MI5, asked me to stop round the corner, not visible from the address. In went the man, to suss out the situation. Now the girl played it real cool and said to me,

"Listen man, are you friends with the police?" I protested my innocence. "I'm in trouble man - real trouble."

With these words she quit the cab and disappeared round the corner into the house. End of Act 1. Pausing, I gathered my scattered wits. Before I had time to check them all back into place, the slim, tall dark glassed man bore down on the cab scowling. "She wants you in there" indicating with his thumb.

With my badge shining brightly, I entered what was once an elegant hallway and now looked like a pram and bike park. "Sorry cabby I cannot pay you, charge it to the phone, will you?". I nearly dropped into the cellar. "Madam" I said, "the fare is payable in cash not in phone numbers".

The client responded by saying "The landlord was going to pay, but he is not here at the moment. Charlie has gone to find him. It will be easy, he is sure to be in one of six pubs". I noticed that long tall Charlie was nowhere to be seen. "Lady, can't one of your friends pay the fare?" I asked. Someone had appeared in each of the doorways round the hall. "Oh no" they said in unison. "It is Monday and we have all run out of money until Friday night".

After the local police with whom I am now acquainted, sorted the matter out, the money was found. It was only the unpaid fare which had kept me there, it was not the ladies' attractions. She had not taken off her dark glasses the entire time. Whenever really dark glasses approach the Cab, I sit and shiver in anticipation.

Waiting at Kings Cross rank on a Wednesday evening after most last trains had departed, a nearly sober man, reasonably dressed, middle aged, asked for Cambridge. I must have pulled a face for he told me he knew what the fare would be and that he had enough money on him to cough up on arrival. We travelled in silence, mile after mile in the blackness of the motorway. I was both excited, for this 'Roader' would make up for a poor week's work, and apprehensive since the fare was so great. Finally, we arrived in the suburbs of the city. I was now directed through the streets and to a block of flats. By this time the alcohol had got to him and he either acted, or actually became belligerent. At this point I realised I had made a mistake. The business-like agreement of Kings Cross was miles away, and I was in a foreign manor. His aggressive talk left me reacting in an equally unfriendly manner.

He said, "Mine is the block with the with the bell on it", but none were to be seen. He then, began querying my lack of knowledge of Cambridge's byways. Already unhappy and in a strange environment, my concern was doubled when he sprinted into the block whist shouting something like "I am getting the cash". Looking at the block from my seat at that time of night, in the small hours, when everyone else was asleep I pinpointed the apartment where he lived.

A light went on. I was easily able to count the floors and the relationship of the light to the stairwell. After a while I took my change bag out of the cab as a precaution but forgot to lock the door and went up after him. After a prolonged session of banging on the door and being told to "....off" I departed for the nearest police station, which I had luckily spotted on the way in. I knew my rights, for to not pay a cab driver is a criminal, as opposed to a civil, offence.

A couple of days later, when I tried to set up a small claims case, I realised that the adage, 'My first loss is my best loss', was true. Time spent in police stations explaining my case was a waste of working hours. I was compounding my loss which was stupid. I made a business like decision and admitted defeat.

Chapter 13
Bilkers & Social Relationships

Many passengers who are sufficiently well-versed in life, know that a driver will not take out a summons for a small unpaid fare, although he is legally entitled to do so. Non-payment of a cab fare is a criminal offence. The passenger knows that it takes a rich man to go to law, so one of the techniques employed after threatening to call the police immediately, is to stand outside the destination of the would-be bilker. Next, the driver can begin to 'dis' the bilker, his family antecedents, the neighbourhood, in fact anything which will bring the matter to a close. Half the purpose is to bring the issue to the attention of the neighbours. This system is often successful.

About 20:00 on a Friday night a woman stopped me in Coventry Street and asked to be driven to Leicester Square Post Office. I explained that it was very close by, and she replied that she was very tired. So, I drove her the 500 yards. She told me to wait while she transacted some business. I waited a minute and then made a guess, jumped out of my driving seat and stood on the pavement right by the Post Officer door. Sure enough, out she came, turned abruptly and started to walk away. I raced after her and she explained,

"I have been paying all my life ….and am not going to pay any more!". Being in the middle of London, I threatened to call a policeman and she agreed that it was a good idea. Then I reached a conclusion - that she wanted to be arrested. I left the taxi and caught up with her. I walked with her from Hippodrome Corner to Leicester Square and we still did not see any officers of the law. At which point I left her to get herself arrested; my meter was running, and I could not afford to pay my boss any more uncollected money which had been accruing on the meter or risk another parking ticket. The police would also have been able to charge me for not being in attendance with my cab.

Saturday afternoon, the sun was shining, and I had just started work. Two women walked out from Old Church Street Chelsea on my left and hailed me, I stopped promptly there on the Kings Road SW3. The first woman helped the second into the cab and immediately left the vicinity. My passenger spoke.

"Can you help me?" I trust I did not wince. Her haggard features combined with a door key pinned safely to the lapel of her well-worn coat, suggested that a social worker might be more appropriate than a cab driver.

"I don't know what to do" she said, "I have just paid for an hotel room and when I returned to the door of the hotel, though it was open, there were no lights on, and I was scared of tripping and then falling. I could not find my room and there was no one there to help me. Perhaps they did not want me to come back till later in the day". She paused for breath, and I wondered how I was supposed to help. She began anew, "Is there a hospital nearby you know, so I will not have to pay too much cab fare to get there?".

I suggested the Chelsea Hospital for Women she asked "Where else" The Royal Marsden was not appropriate as it was a cancer hospital, but I suggested one with an Outpatients Department. En route to the Brompton Hospital – the one we had settled on – she related to me that she had a headache and might fall on her own indoors. I brought her to the Outpatients Department of the Brompton and assured her that there would be someone inside to help her and departed quickly.

Mood change. I have to admit the next person who hailed me was exciting to look at. Calculatingly enticing, and I am a healthy young man. Her well-groomed hair was smooth, a lustrous black, soft and silky, immaculately brushed it culminated in a sinuous plait resting on her shoulders. Her bosom was scarcely restrained by her all too flimsy bra and even flimsier blouse. Her skirt succeeded in projecting the contours of her hips and legs. I stopped the cab next to her with what I hoped, was a virile flourish. She was totally unaware I was prepared to drive like a demon on her behalf. "Queensway, dear" she said and hopped into the cab, absolutely ignoring all the gigolos and spectators as we left Dean Street in Soho. She was oblivious of me I thought. "Got a match love?" she asked in a homely north country accent. Good for her. "How are you miss?" I enquired gallantly. How we started our conversation I do not know, but I must admit she needed little prompting to continue. It needed few questions from me to elicit her life story.

Convinced she had swallowed a rather blue novel, I listened to each word spoken in her Yorkshire accent, while we travelled between Soho and Bayswater. Her tale began with her leaving the Shires and coming to London to make her fortune. All seemed to have gone well with her. She was apparently successful, and then one day she had an offer. A girl of her outgoing temperament found the offer irresistible and off she went, to continue her career as an entertainer in Paris. She lived and worked in France and once again all went well, until one day she witnessed a stabbing in Montmartre. Having told the details and inadvertently given the description of the attacker to the interrogating gendarme, it became clear that her description was all too accurate, and the police knew the offender. The assailant was a member of a mafia type group who were not happy with this intervention into their private affairs.

So off she set again, this time for Marseilles. From there it was but a short hop to Algiers. And so, her story continued. In the end, of course, she returned to her first love: Soho. This history, which was a film waiting to be made, was related to me within a six shilling journey.

One busy Saturday night a woman appeared, hailed me, jumped into the cab and asked to driven to the nearest milk vending machine to buy a bottle of milk. Watching her slipping the money into the slot, I noticed that before the coin had entered the mechanism, two or three cars had pulled up with their engines still running and several male pedestrians watched her closely until she returned to the safety of my cab. The whirl of excitement dissipated. I drove her back to her home.

I was on point at Victoria Station when an elderly woman in an ill-fitting blouse and open coat approached the cab and asked for the 'Elephant' (and Castle) SE1, I watched her get in and wondered if her worn out shopping bag would split. It did not. It was around six in the evening, and I was a little upset to go South of the river at this time of night. As we cleared the southern side of Vauxhall Bridge she suddenly asked if I would take her to Ilford IG1. This too was an unwelcome destination, as it entailed fighting all the way across London during the rush hour. I was uncertain that I had heard the question correctly. I had a feeling that this untidily dressed lady might not pay me. The abrupt change from

South to North London unsettled me. "Do it at 'excursion' rate" she kidded me.

To deter her and cover my time in getting back to West London, I asked the full fare. A journey longer than 6 miles can be priced, and includes the return journey under the then, Hackney Carriage Acts. She accepted the price. As we were already south of the river, I had to begin to devise routes to avoid possible traffic congestion. Having made my decisions, I tried to ascertain a few facts. "Where about in Ilford do you want?" My knowledge of that area was limited. "I'll tell you when we get there" she replied,

"The Broadway?" A landmark I knew. "No, Valentine's Park in Cranbrook Road." A clear enough answer to calm any doubts.

"Live near there, do you?" keeping the conversation running. No, I'm a hobo" with a cheerful chuckle. "Visiting friends?". By now I was more than a little disconcerted. "No, I just want to see the park".

All of this was happening at 18:00 in the dark, for it was late autumn, and believe it or not, it was raining. I was a little disturbed at her words

"I am a Hobo", or was she really one? Added to the fact she wanted to see the park at night, I began to sweat a little. I made the decision that as soon as she defaulted on payment I would call the police, but for now I would continue conversing with her and leave it at that; in fact, I could detect no ill purpose in her.

The talk continued and she bemoaned the change from the 'old days' to the 'present', the absence of the gracious living with its attendant personal attention. She side tracked into berating the change into decimal coinage. She summed it up in one sentence: "Mr. Wilson has no right to do it – none at all."

We reached Valentine's Park at 18:30, which I suggest to you, was a testament to my driving skills. I drove slowly down Cranbrook Road while my passenger looked eagerly into the shadows of the dark sullen, night time park. Trees lashing their leafless branches futilely into the falling rain. She peered at everything we passed soaking in the atmosphere rather than the depths of the black scenery. She said that some of the trees were gone, but not too many. I put two and two together. We drove onwards towards Gants Hill, she, watching the houses the shops, the bricks. The viewing of the park took an entire four minutes with me driving as slowly as safely possible.

She told me then, we could return. I replied that it would be appropriate if she would pay me for the journey so far. She did so, commenting that I was a suspicious person. I then offered to restart the clock so it would be running at the cheaper rate. She agreed. Back we went again, she still imbibing the streets, avenues, and houses, while denigrating the new fashions. I listened and concentrated on the traffic. The chit chat revealed she had spent some £4,000 in the last several years travelling all over London on just this kind of trip. We arrived back in Victoria at 19:15. During the moments when she left the cab, I noticed that the coat she was wearing so haphazardly, was either a real or imitation Persian Lamb and the watch on her wrist was not inexpensive. All in all, I think that was the most eccentric journey I have ever completed. I tried to create a rational explanation for the trip, and the best I could do was that she was visiting old haunts from earlier in her life. Nostalgia at work?

Even if someone is polite and well mannered, there is never a guarantee that he will play fair. One evening, a 20-year-old approached me politely and asked if I would take a cheque. I agreed, and we duly arrived at the destination. There I was presented with a cheque made out to "Prince B..." for £5, and was asked for £4 change. I refused to give him change but accepted the cheque. Next day I attempted to pay in the cheque and the clerk asked me if I were a member of his (Prince B's) gang. At length the bank explained that the cheque had to be submitted by the person to whom it was made out.

I went to the police station with the cheque and was told that he was just within the law. Having lost an hour at the bank and the police station, I remembered that 'My first loss ...' and forgot the matter. Later, this character was arrested in Cornwall for obtaining a BEA air ticket fraudulently. Once again, I had gambled and lost, but the temptation of £5 for a £1 journey was too great.

It was not more than a month after the previous incident, that the driver in front of me on the South Kensington rank rejected a client and pointed the punter back towards me. I was interested to know why he had declined the job. The woman in her thirties, thin but not wan, handsome looking, approached me smiling. She was well dressed, no way a pauper.

As she spoke her voice was smoky, and not so long ago might have been husky seductive. Today, it was merely the sound that embraced me. "I want Cornwall Gardens" just round the corner. Nothing wrong there. "I live on the second floor, and I want to move some luggage to Chelsea". Anyway, I fell for the story; I was second in line and who knows how long I might have had to wait for the next job.

This was one of those slight variations of work which are the prelude to an interesting job. "Hop in" I said to her. Luckily Cornwall Gardens was wide, and was a residential non through road, so I was able to double park. Up we went to the second floor. As we climbed the stairs, she related that she was changing digs the next day but was taking only half of her gear now, as the new room was not completely ready.

The stairs were steep, and the flat was high up. As we reached the landing she gasped in surprise. At least I think it was in surprise. All her possessions had been pushed into the hall. She dithered, apparently uncertain what had happened. I started to select 3 cases to carry down. At this point the landlady suddenly appeared. "You should have been out by midday". It was now 14:00. "I have your radio safely downstairs" she continued. She was stern, dour and definitely inflexible. The description offered by the rider later, was that the housekeeper was shanty park material. If this was a shanty, I would have liked to have owned a fraction. We packed the cab full and drove off to the estate agent to demand an explanation as to the precise dates involved. She showed me a document which clearly stated the morrow as the end of her lease.

"Please, now drive me to Lots Road, I want a street near there". We found it and began the process of offloading the gear. Cases, hangers, hat boxes, grips etc. I noted there were none of the carrier bags and boxes that I usually come across with this type of 'flit'. Off we went again, the passenger seemingly indefatigable, asked me what I would do about it, the lost day's tenancy. I replied that she should forget it.

I expounded my *'first loss is best loss'* theory. When she explained she worked as an office receptionist, I responded that competition was no doubt fierce. I began to feel uneasy, as she was talking too much, seemingly in a quandary as to what to do next. I suggested she drank a cup of coffee. "I prefer beer, would you like to join me while the pubs are still open?". An hour having elapsed on this move, digs to digs I knew I had spent too long on this job. I declined. It put her out a little. She paid me well. I circled the block looking for my next passenger and was still empty 10 minutes later, when I noticed this same lady strolling seemingly aimlessly towards a bus stop.

Usually young females are good tippers, some when travelling on their own are friendly and others remote. There are those who I suspect feel that they are moving up in the world to enter a taxi, and try to speak well, to impress me. But when asked a question in the course of conversation, they revert to their normal tones and give the game away.

It is usually safe to drive females, so I was unprepared when a quintet jumped in and asked for a block of flats in Streatham. The precise final location was down a ramp beneath a block, and it was there where I was told to stop. I did this, only to experience both passenger doors being flung open simultaneously. And, five sets of laughter and giggles, as they raced away in different directions without payment of the fare. Then one of the girls came sprinting back as she had left her handbag. I slammed the doors shut by driving forwards and breaking, the double momentum rammed the doors closed, and then I drove forward again this time to the local nick. I went inside with the purse and told the duty officer what had happened, and said I did not intend to press charges. But, when someone came to reclaim the handbag, the Bill should read them the riot act. I think I left the building smiling to myself. It was an audacious end to their night out.

The debate, who encounters the greatest hardship on losing his or her spouse – widower or widow, had until the following events seemed to me to be somewhat academic. It is the temperament and capability of the survivor that triumphs in the end. A widower might wander around asking pathetically "How often should I be changing my socks?". A widow for the first weeks, harshly becomes aware that the budget *must* balance, and there is no one to turn to. Age, finance and family are the criteria of the situation. Ultimately it is a person's ability to cope – or not – that determines the rest of his or her life.

I was driving down Wellington Road, St. John's Wood NW4. and was hailed. The sun was shining, the punter was standing at a bus stop heading South (into town where I wanted to be) and I anticipated an uncomplicated job. But one never knows.

She was wearing a matching fur jacket and hat and had a suitcase with a tightly furled umbrella tucked neatly alongside the handle. My rapid glance assessed her to be about 50 years old, and she had an aura of neatness about her. She asked for Westbourne Park Road. I grunted a thank you and started the drive. I had the impression she was unused to London Taxis, for she gave me the address from inside the cab. Perhaps that was because she had to read it from a letter. The journey began by traversing the least salubrious part of Kilburn. Street after street of decaying dilapidated houses, some with conspicuously boarded windows and doors. Grey facades of peeling paint and crumbling masonry. The woman leaned forward and enquired – I thought a trifle anxiously – "Are we heading to W2?" (the postal District). I assured her we were, though I was not sure myself. Later looking at an A-Z map I noticed that the destination road runs from the dubious W11 to W2.

Once over a canal bridge we came to the road. I saw immediately that we had entered W11 and hoped that my fare's eyes were not as quick as mine. This part of the road, just as the roads we had recently driven through boasted multiple, rental occupied houses. Each window flew a different coloured curtain, if curtains were there at all. Washing exposed to the light of day, or perhaps the light of the sun, appeared in every other window. Dozens of full and empty milk bottles littered doorstep after doorstep. We continued further, coming abruptly as one does in London from W11 to W2. Then as the road curved, the tenor of the road changed. Some of the houses had been painted in the last 5 years, a positive sign, and here seemed as if they could have been divided into apartments rather than bedsitter rooms.

We came to the house, a smallish one, which could have been occupied by a single family. The garden in front, in keeping with the others, was a miniature jungle of weeds run wild. The woman started to pay me off, when abruptly, she had misgivings.

"You couldn't wait a quarter hour for me, could you?". Experience has taught me that 15 minutes quickly turns into 30. Whilst I was trying to formulate a courteous refusal it became clear I did not have change for the £1 note she was offering me. At that moment a man approached. "Are you Mr. Smith? ….. would you pay the taxi for me?". Quite amazingly, Mr. Smith had no change either, and even more disconcertingly, he suggested I toddle up the road to the local shops to get some. He commented "Don't worry we will still be here". This was the first time in 8 years of driving I have been sent off by someone to find some change. While driving away in search of change, I noted Mr. Smith pull a bottle of milk from his pocket with considerable expertise. I popped into the local dairy, and in here the female behind the counter was having to hold her own with the added presence of a massive Alsatian – against a couple of men. The argument dissolved as I interposed myself between them. The men reluctantly left.

Having obtained the change, I returned to the house. Seeing me return, Mr. Smith called my lady to pay me off. Whilst she searched for her purse my quick glance indoors showed the stairs lacked covering – no carpet or even lino. My fare whispered to me, once again to wait for her, and even as she spoke the words, she made a rapid decision to depart immediately. She hustled herself and her case into the taxi and we left post haste. Sensing a drama, I enquired if anything was amiss. Then in broken out of sequence phrases, she told me that she was recently bereaved and was looking for employment.

An Agency in Kent had sent her here, but she guessed she would not only have to look after 2 children, but she might well have to provide for them as well (I wondered what problems Mr. Smith was facing himself). She wanted a position where she would drive, rather than be a governess, but the set-up there that afternoon was too frightful. She decided to leave the matter in abeyance for a couple of months, while she continued to live with her daughter in Kent. Maybe something more promising would turn up in the future. I hoped so for her sake.

My very last ride that same afternoon was a woman who exited a fashionable Mayfair apartment and asked to be driven to Bloomsbury. "I trust you will not be surprised at the difference in addresses". I commented that nothing surprised me anymore. The latest passenger was a 60-year-old, a nurse companion to an ailing lady. For the last 14 days she had not left the flat, but now she had this chance to 'go out' as her employer had gone away to the country. She philosophised on the lot of a widow and the capricious nature of life. She continued, that it was happy people like cabdrivers and the porters at Dover (she was European) that made her love Britain. "Obviously my patient is not able to joke with me…however, I will be able to retire within a couple of years" she added philosophically.

Life, it seemed to me had not overwhelmed her. Neither woman (my earlier and my latest passenger) was living an easy life, but both were attempting to come to terms with the situation into which they had arbitrarily been thrown. Similar problems obviously exist for other persons suddenly left fending for themselves.

One day an American tourist requested "The Sherlock Holmes" in Baker Street. I was not perturbed because I know that many pub names are duplicated. En route I reconsidered the request, and we settled for the Sherlock Holmes Pub in Northumberland Street. He wondered where he had gained the impression that it was in Baker Street. I dryly replied, "You must have been reading!". Others who know the Conan Doyle series are based on Baker Street ask to be driven past his house. When this piece was written the museum had not yet been created.

Visitors from the United States have a unique variety of English-isms. Not only do they dispense with "Please" or "Thank you", but also save breath by omitting 'Street, Road, Avenue or Gardens'. This system is clearly admirable when used thus: "Time and Life on Bruton and Bond". It is in fact superior to normal English usage.

But one Wednesday night when a group were on an overnight stay in London and wanted to return to their hotel, they asked me for the Gloucester Hotel in Queensgate. I said "OK", convinced I could find any hotel on Queensgate no matter how small, for Queensgate SW7 is not long. However, after driving up and down Queensgate three times, I decided to look up the Hotel in the phone book in the nearest phone box and discovered that it was not listed. I stopped at a variety of hotels the length of the street, and no one could help me. Suddenly I had a brainwave. I realised they wanted Queensgate Gardens W2, and they had asked for one of the few thoroughfares in London without an addendum. To add to the confusion, they were staying at the Leicester Court Hotel. I do not believe that they had had too much to drink. They and I were relieved to find the hotel was still there, and in the end, there were no ill feelings.

A similar enigmatic address was given to me by a tousle haired youth who required 75, Stoke Newington. Everyone knows that Number 1 London is Apsley House. And that Albany, London, is a private road off Piccadilly. I did not believe there was anything of this nature in North London. My passenger could not help or describe the street, because he had only that day moved in, and what was more, could not recognise the house from the outside because he had to traverse an alley to reach his front door. The choices were few, Stoke Newington Road, Stoke Newington Common, Stoke Newington Church Street, and SN High Street, all of which were N16. We quickly struck lucky on the second try, and the young man made his way down the appropriate alley to his home.

In a similar manner, the local shop, restaurant, store, or what have you, has a local nickname and is well known to the riders who live in the vicinity. It is not one of the landmarks recognised on the Knowledge. So, the familiar description is fairly pointless and frustrating to both parties. The diminutive adjective 'Little' often gives the game away and spoils the game, but while the driver is accustomed to this line of conversation, it remains a constant irritant on a bad day.

Sometimes a journey is of two parts, and the vast majority of punters have the courtesy to state this either at the start or en route. This variation to a normal job might entail a wait, but there is a school which refuses to divulge the secret until the last minute. On one occasion a couple jumped into the cab and asked to be taken to Earl's Court Road. We arrived and as usual, I stopped the clock as I have previously been berated for the meter clocking an extra thruppence. Sadly, the female, exited the cab and I was next instructed to drive to Kensington High Street which I did. This involved me driving illegally, as the meter was in the stopped position and therefore could be construed as not working. I wonder if the Insurance was effective and similarly, I was depriving the cab owner of the time element in the fare. Truly, the distance was clocking up but not the time.

To ask for the fare and restart the clock would be making the rider pay twice the 'Fall of Clock' rate for the first distance. Arriving at Ken. High Street after I had stretched my shoulder and hand through the window to receive the fare, I was told the man was popping into the 'Off' to buy a couple of bottles of plonk.

To my relief, the store was empty, so it only took 8 minutes to choose. At last, we arrived in Stafford Street W1. This had been mentioned as the end of the journey. There, I was informed some paintings were to be collected and then we would continue. I refused, complaining that the contract had been broken twice and I was already out of pocket as no time having been recorded for payment, since the clock does not register time once stopped. I was unprepared to wait a third time and not be paid, for yet a further period. The journey ended there, with an amicable conclusion, in that I was both paid and given a good tip.
Once I had to take the can back. But I was pleased – for someone had run out of fuel and had bought a gallon of petrol, then let me take the can back and retrieve the deposit.

Yes, there are other good times too. Whilst I was waiting for a passenger to do some shopping - with the meter running - I was gazing wistfully at some cigars in the tobacconist's window adjacent to where I was parked. Then the passenger, who had completed his shopping, returned and caught me staring. He entered the shop and bought me a cigar as a thank you present! This passenger turned out to be a gentleman.

That same night, in the dark, I was urged to take payment from my fare's hand, which was a trick glove in the shape of an ape's hand. It was covered with fur and had the sharpest claws. I nearly abandoned the money and drove away for help. He was for sure, no gentleman.

One night at the 'Angel' (Islington) a trio of well-dressed women asked to be taken to "Bill's Caff". I know some of the pull-ins in the South West but I am not conversant with those in Holloway Road N7. I let them direct me. I still could not reconcile pearls and fashionable dress with a coffee shop, nevertheless we arrived. I read the name on the fascia, and it was 'Beal's Restaurant', a large well established restaurant in Holloway. I realised then that I should have known it.

November 5, 1962, I was driving past the House of Commons when I saw three fire engines driving close to Palace Yard. Only one went in, and I thought maybe history was about to repeat itself. I dashed to a phone box, and tried to convince the copy room of several newspapers that there was a repetition of history, but no one was interested. They did not even think it was amusing.

November 6 the next day, when I had a job to Houses of Parliament, I discovered that a prankster had phoned the Fire Brigade and said that there was a fire in the boiler room in the House of Commons. It was actually, not a real fire but the central heating boiler doing its job.

Pageantry and splendour are of course tradition, and that is the real reason the complicated and not inexpensive traffic lights on Parliament Square are not used when our Parliament is sitting. Tradition dictates the MPs have the right of way to attend the House when it is in session. The Point Policeman is supposed to recognise and salute an MP. The traffic lights find the task of saluting difficult. Thus, unless the House is in recess, the traffic lights do not operate, and quite a few policemen are employed controlling the crossing at additional cost to the public purse. Recent attacks, post 1963, have proved the police presence to be more necessary than previously thought.
It took me over a year to discover that the electric bulb winking in one of the stone columns on the corner of Bridge Street and Parliament

Square, was a request for an empty taxi to enter. It took me much less time to discover that MPs were either badly paid or did not tip well. One MP to whom this does not apply, told me how much he admired taxi drivers, and that he represented our interests in the Commons. Driving onwards in the course of the ensuing conversation, the passenger and I discovered, that we were both housed by the same landlord, and he told me that they would never sell out to a take-over bid. I warmed to his words for my rent was reasonable. Some two years later I started a conversation with a different person, and within minutes I recognised that I had heard these words before, and realised it was the same MP. I recalled our previous conversation, and it turned out that we both had new landlords – the previous property owner having sold to various developers. He bemoaned the fact, relating that he must leave his premises soon, as the new rent was now too high. The subject changed, and he reverted to his original theme of "The Gentlemen of the Road". I trust he was not referring to Highway Robbers.

Chapter 14
Seasonal Work Variations

It was a chilly mid-November night, and at last, a trio has hailed me. "Yes Sir, the Pad". I guessed he had brought the girls in to see the Christmas lights. They are much the same this year as last. Oh No! I think to myself, even a window display of Christmas greetings from a company that kills woodworm, tins of poison, are covered in holly and wrapped in ribbons. Would the economy of the country exist without the fantastic sales of goods at this time of year? So many Christmas trees about, festooned in little lights; how thoughtful of them to make the top light white, and not coloured. In some of the council blocks there are displays in nearly every front window. I stop for the traffic lights here and next I stop for the traffic lights opposite the park. Just watch the wind spin these leaves about: one minute a whirlwind whisking them into a cone, now a gust and they are all scampering about, scurrying along the ground as if playing 'catch'. I think I will turn the heater on full. "That will be 3 and 9 pence please Sir, thanks very much."

Taxi work is not only seasonal work, but it has daily peaks. There are hours that it is not worth being out. A prime example is Christmas day. I learned that the hard way. Bright and early, I went on the streets and nary a bird was to be seen. Convinced that there would be work in the centre of town, my dismay reached new bounds, when I discovered nothing in Central London was open. I had to retreat through empty streets to suburban neighbourhoods, where I discovered a steady trickle of punters trekking to family for the annual feed up. I got it. But it did take a couple of years before I learned to leave home around teatime. The more years I worked the more obvious it became.

It is Christmas day, and most drivers are at home enjoying their turkey meal and I am in a situation where I can pick and choose my punters. Naturally, I choose only those that can remain vertical. I slowed for a fellow, and then noted that his two companions are holding one another up. I come to the rapid conclusion that if one of the party, were to be sick in the cab, that would cost me my night's work. I ignore them and cross to the far side of the road to pick up a single pin who can hold himself upright. As he is entering the cab, out of the blue, the tipsy giant who had hailed me a few seconds earlier lumbers across the road and starts to punch me from where he stood. He punctuates the blows with the explanation that I should have stopped for him. Discretion was called for, I hastily depart the scene cursing for the next half hour, and nursing a sore nose.

I wonder if this Christmas will be the same as last year. I need not have surmised – I know for sure it will be. I will be driving a cab throughout the Bank Holiday in order to pay for my Christmas break during the quiet, slow month of January.

Last year's big chuckle will not, I fear, be repeated, or even equalled this year. It is an eloquent request "It is impossible to live this night without meat… you know?" I would that I could turn as pretty a phrase if I was as hungry on Christmas night in a foreign country. With no sign of emaciation or even exhaustion on their smooth, well-rounded countenances, it is with grateful thanks the European couple charm me with their sincere gratitude for my great kindness, in finding them a restaurant which was open on this Christmas day in London's West End.

Christmas Eve, I feel just as much the good fellow when I do not run over the character who left the pavement backwards and continued in a straight line to the far side of the road. His progress was doubly unusual in that his head and shoulders preceded the remainder of his body, successfully defying gravity for all of the 30 feet. The driver approaching from the other side of the road also saved this *'acrobat's life'*, but was more than disturbed when gravity finally won, and pulled the character down in front of his car. He pulled up; I drive on. I have much to do. I have both seen and anticipate witnessing many more such sights.

Meanwhile in South Kensington, as every year, there are the usual multitudes of smartly dressed worshippers on their way to enjoy the traditional Christmas Eve Midnight Service in Brompton Oratory SW3. It is a fashionable sight, yet somehow it clicks in my head that this is how it might have been in Victorian days. Calm and dignity shine through the slight bustle.

Still December 24th I am in Ladbroke Grove W11. Pushing on into Chamberlayne Road W13 a man fretfully blunders against the door of a laundromat which claims that it is open 24 hours every day. He is frustrated, and I suppose he had every right to be – the door is locked. He carries no washing, but who wants to wash clothes on Christmas Eve? He is clearly not to be placated by reasoning. Soon I am taken out towards Harlesden NW10. It seems that the unruliness plague has struck here. Or is it that the Pubs are now disgorging their clients?

The streets are littered with men who know not where they are, what the time is, or even what day it is. They are sick, vomiting into the street and reeling in their excesses. I had forgotten previous years, and am thus surprised that the Pubs are open until 23:30, but I honestly should have known better. I should have remembered what happened last year. All it means is that I will now have to circumspectly stop 10 yards away from anyone who hails me. Then, and only then, will I be able to see if the would-be passenger, can pursue a straight line towards me, and I can allow him to ride in my puritanical taxi.

Rounding the next corner, I see ranks of parked cars, in serried lines that are awaiting their drivers and passengers; they are outside the local church. A pleasant festive vision.

A tree with twinkling, coloured lights, in the icy December air, combines to build the festive ambience. The church's grey stone walls and tower are floodlit for all to see. I enjoy this sight. It is a reminder of the day, and oddly similar to the many cards we have received over the past week that are tonight adorning our mantelpiece.

The contrast between the two groups of residents – drinkers and prayers – in this neighbourhood of North London gives me pause to think, and whoops, I nearly make an error. I anticipated cars coming round that corner at 30 mph. I forgot that they can do 60 mph on Christmas Eve. I had better not make another error like that. Somehow, I am now in Greenford UB6, after a series of jobs has pulled me further and further West. Now in front of me is another fine modern church, all the more handsome with the illuminated interior percolating and projecting bright light outwards, bringing vivid vitality to the fresh architectural styling. I suspect that many of the devout leaving the building are rarely out of doors so late at night. The majority are elderly, dressed up against the cold in their Christmas best. I am about to set a fare down in Acton NW10, when I notice a man supporting himself fast asleep on the sand-bin, which is available to remedy icy wintery roads.

I ask my passenger's permission to stop round the corner, in case the man wakes and hails me. I reverse round a corner out of sight. Then come a series of jobs up and down Horn Lane Acton, most passengers having come from Church. Some of them must be once-a-year riders. I spend about ½ hour at this kind of work. Up and down the road.

At the end of this time, the man at the sand bin has managed to wake sufficiently to move forward and hang onto the nearest park railing. All in all, he is moving three yards in half an hour. In his state, he deserves hearty congratulations.

I conclude my Christmas working stint on Boxing Day. My January holiday is on my mind, but there were a few more workdays left in December, including New Year's Eve. Naturally, the next few days work will be conventional. Sure enough, they are. On Thursday I was stopped at Charing Cross Road WC2, and asked in all seriousness by a woman "What time is early closing, in Leytonstone E10?" I do not thank her for hailing me and making me stop for nothing.

New Year's Eve, my wife and I arrived at the party by underground, and had a whale of a time, and then we had to find a cab to return home. I used my expertise to walk on the correct side of the road, in order to catch a cab travelling in our direction. There were not many, and all those that passed us were occupied. At last, we saw a cab with its For Hire sign on. We hailed it and it flew past us. Finally, I understood the frustration of the jilted traveller as empty taxis with lights blazing fly passed him. Later on, we found a cab and arrived home safely.

I had reasoned working over the Christmas period the public would appreciate taxis, and that I would then rest when there was a dearth of work. The 'Kipper Season', the first weeks of the New Year, are perhaps the quietest of the year, so I usually take time off in January. Returning from my rest, the garage was still there, squashed between the undertakers and the second-hand shop. Once down the cab's width alley between the shops, the route enlarged into the garage. I tried not to slip on the winter's black ice that had formed in the week I had been resting. Cabs departing the garage after the nightly wash, drip water which ultimately turns to ice on the wooden blocks. I am not an actor, but drivers too receive no pay if they are not working, so I can legitimately say 'I am resting'.

Having previously phoned in to say I was ready to start work, I checked in with my usually genial boss, that my regular cab was available, but was greeted brusquely, as he did not want to change his mood. He was listening to the account of a cab driver who had bashed in the front of the cab he was driving. I scurried out of the office, I did not want to be involved in any way, certainly not to hear the details. I approached my cab, circled it to make sure there was no visible damage and dumped my torch, gear, maps, change and a nosh into the cab. I then read the meter so that when I finished the shift, I could calculate how many 'falls of clock' and how many 'units' had been registered, and pay in accordingly.

I jumped into the cab and threw out the collection of match boxes and the week old newspapers, which had accumulated from the previous driver, and made sure that my collection of road maps had not disappeared. I began to reverse the cab out of its parking spot- it felt like a lorry – I had driven a private car during my holiday. The car I had driven now seemed as if it had wings as light as a daisy, but it did not have the awesome aspect of the cab, which perhaps allows me to gain right of way. Occasionally when driving the cab, I waive this right, and beckon with beneficence and magnanimity for motorists and pedestrians to cross in front of me. Unfortunately, I was unable to utilise some of the more primitive forms of bluffing that I so enjoy, while I was 'resting', but now I would be able to do so driving in my public service vehicle. Sadly, few will automatically give way to a little private car, like my holiday transport. Occasionally when driving today many years after retirement I need to be reminded by my wife that I am no longer in charge of a taxi.

I filled the tank with diesel, left the garage, and crossed the river Thames via Chelsea Bridge heading for Sloane Square SW1. While waiting at a traffic light the road behind me suddenly began leaping with each gust of wind. The last alcohol I had consumed was days ago on New Year's Eve, so something else was amiss. Then I realised what was happening: the mirror attached to my front wing was flapping. If I had been driving the cab, I would have had it tightened immediately; the driver who had used the cab while I was away had simply not bothered to report it.

There was a period of my career when I drove around with a camera handy. I had given this habit up, when not long into the New Year one

Tuesday it happened. I had nearly arrived home for lunch, as I was then on day work, when I noticed a small bubble car which had run over and up a load of goods shed from a lorry. This occurred while taking the corner nearest to Battersea Dogs Home under the railway bridge. The bubble was on its side, and I thought that this would make a good picture. So, I rushed to the nearest chemist in Battersea Park Road SW11. I had finished the film in my camera which was at home anyway, and had as yet, not removed it. Entering the shop, I found that a little girl was buying nail polish, and the sales assistant was being very attentive to her. Eventually, I bought the film and sped home to our flat in a mansion block facing Battersea Park.

I was sweating freely from the rush, and gasped out to my wife what I had seen and what I intended to do. I loaded the camera and raced back to the cab and drove to the scene of the accident. Only, to be held up by the policeman who was by now directing traffic around the accident site. At last, I parked, jumped out of the cab, and took my precious photo. I raced home and started to phone the evening papers. No one was interested, unless there had been a fatality. This was a mundane daily occurrence. Determined to get a result, I knocked on the neighbour's door and found out the name of the local paper. This paper would not commit itself but promised to look at my prints; they did in the end publish a photo. The time and energy involved were scarcely commensurate with the reward and the honour. However, I have since made a practice that if any tourist is taking a photo and I am passing by, to lean out of the window and give an ear-to-ear grin.

I guess my photo is probably in hundreds of tourists' photo albums in front of most of London's monuments and most famous buildings. That is if I have not broken the lenses of their cameras.

Chapter 15
London Traffic

There was a time when London's road gutters were used mainly to let rainwater flow to the drains. Then in the mid-60s that changed, and there was a frenzied spate of painting and decorating them with striped yellow lines (namely, No Parking Here signs). So today in place of a dirty grey patina, the roadsides are a jaundiced yellow. Currently we are in the midst of the largest painting and coloured cement exercise London has ever seen. I am not counting the Yellow Plague of 1664. Yellow stripes, either single or double, indicate that there is no parking permitted. However, once a vehicle is on a yellow line, he cannot see it. To remedy this, the line grows tendrils which slither upwards onto the curb towards the paving stones. The pedestrians do not trip on them and the driver has a better chance to see where he should and should not be.

Then came diagonals, and squeezed chess boards, defying drivers to remain stationary at a crossroads; each driver has to guess what the vehicles before him have decided, or an error will leave him stranded midstream. To stay still or move on? I have recently been pipped at the post by a Stirling Moss, the racing driver of the 1960s, or could it have been Lewis Hamilton who managed to whizz into the precise unmarked part of the road I was aiming at. The obvious result … a fine. I was caught meandering on the yellow chequer board. If only there were hoods like criminals' wear, to conceal vehicle number plates. White cement arrows are today on trial as direction indicators, and the ensuing decades have proved them to be an essential traffic control. We are to this day blessed with 'Red Routes' which forbid stopping/parking. The red paint followed as an afterthought.

The concept of Bus Lanes and allowing taxis use of them, was not yet fully applied, and so the drivers of homeward bound private cars did not have the irritation they have today, of sitting in a jam and watching the taxis move to the front of the queue.

Our metropolitan roads are today an obstacle course. They will remain so, until the traffic or the pedestrians move on different levels. This probably, will never happen as the rising exhaust fumes will choke the walkers on an upper level. Since this was originally written and the implementation of ULEZ *(Ultra Low Emission Zone)*, there has been some short term change for the better.

I never know if there is a policeman or two, waiting to catch the driver who ignores the pedestrians trying to use a Zebra Crossing. Rereading these words some 60 years later, I smile, thinking of the multitude of traffic cameras which grow and flourish right across London. Cameras or not, bobbies on duty occasionally appear. The yellow and red paint on the ground, indicate hazards for the driver and his illicit temptations to park, pick up or drive in a forbidden area. Today, all silently presided over by the omnipresent closed-circuit camera. This is a warning. Driver beware!

This initiative succeeds in its design, for every foot of road surface is being used to its maximum. The vehicular authorities decide the number of lanes of traffic a road will safely hold and mark the tarmac accordingly. London drivers, being London drivers, are inclined to ignore the majority of these markings, yet the closer their cars approach traffic lights, the more obedient the driver. Traffic may wander across all three lanes while racing to get there, yet when they approach and settle at the lights, they find the appropriate 'Get Set' starting positions. The lane markings on the pavement side of the road are frequently ignored, mainly by delivery vans and frequently by shoppers, popping in and out, hogging the space. Something will have to happen apropos of deliveries, and if not, private cars, will imitate the vans and ignore the paint. Respect for the yellow lines grows before traffic lights. The white arrows are ultimately essential, especially where the driving area narrows, and three lanes become two or even one. These markings control the traffic without human intervention. Equally important, the markings indicate directions that are permissible, and those that are closed. They are invaluable.

On those rare moments when there is negligible traffic movement, I am able to be more aware of road surfaces. When they obtain my full attention there are two types of road surface. Roads which have been worn away with constant use by every type of wheeled transport, and are in need of immediate repair. The second type of road surface is where the road has been worked on and the repair join is poor. There is a shudder which vibrates the length of the vehicle as the four wheels cross its perimeter. I can number count on one hand where the road surface remains as smooth as the day it was put down, a year or so on.

The hodgepodge of squares and oblongs created after roadworks make a fairground ride seem smooth. The repair patterns are well suitable for hopscotch but each, creates a juddering trial for travelling vehicles and passengers. This is the secondary nuisance, the prime being the lengthy hold ups until sub surface repairs are finished. Why not reroute the sewers, gas, water pipes, under the pavement when the opportunity arrives. Thus, the noise of trucks bouncing over the hobbled road and the discomforts would be discontinued, and only those old fashioned enough to use Shanks' Pony will suffer.

It has been said that Central London will never be subject to the *absolute ultimate* traffic jam. Traffic will never, grind to an eight-hour standstill.

It could occur in other more modern designed cities, where the roads are laid out so that crossroads intersect at ninety degrees, but in our city with its multitude of side streets running off at tangents it is unlikely to happen. Not only because London with few symmetrical blocks of buildings, does not suffer the classical situation where the tail of one stream obstructs and locks the forward flow of another. This does not arise frequently here, sometimes because of the side streets, there is the opportunity for one car to turn off and in turn, release traffic flow (traffic planners in the 21st century with the aid of cameras and computers and the yellow criss-crosses at road junctions, have a greater control than ever before). They can anticipate and adjust vehicular movements and are able to instantly relay on the radio and roadside screens, news of blockages caused by accidents and collisions. Drivers are additionally informed before they approach a major delay by these illuminated messages. Indeed, nowadays the authorities give advance warnings of future day or night road works. In the 21st century, with Sat Nav, there are numerous apps available that navigate in 'real time', something I would never have dreamed of when I wrote the original text.

In the 60s and 70s alongside the river Thames, there were a couple of road projects. The first was an underpass for the northern end of Blackfriars Bridge, and the second was of road widening upstream, opposite the new Vickers Building. Both efforts are reclaiming land from the river. A Thames clearway would solve the problem and let traffic cross London East to West without stopping and starting many times. Chelsea to Blackfriars has the potential to be such a route. 2022 shows that bicycles have been given precedence over other transport, sometimes slowing traffic speed to a walking pace. Nowadays an abhorrence of exhaust fumes coupled with pedestrian safety, dictate a reduced road speed in order that Londoners are able to breath fresher air.

The City of London prohibitions of wheeled traffic, excluding London Transport buses at Bank Junction, plus speed limits of 20 mph added to bus only roads, are designed to make life more tolerable for City Workers (2023). 2023 suggested that parts of Oxford Street should be pedestrian, and pavements could be widened. The Congestion Charge is credited with ameliorating the number of private cars in the centre of town.

The tidal flow of motor vehicles on Chelsea Bridge is determined daily by the usual quantity of traffic at a given time of day. Additionally, permanent One-Way systems on the Albert and Battersea Bridges, are interesting, but are they long-term solutions? I am, even as I type this, aware that the better the traffic flow the more cars will each day drill their way into this immense metropolis. In the 21st Century the closure of Hammersmith Bridge affects the daily lives of local residents and long-distance drivers. Cyclists are permitted to cross, but persons that use buses face a real dilemma.

In recent years those imbecilic jams caused by two directions of right turning traffic interlocking, have been happening less frequently. In 2023, a right turn is made *in front of* the opposing turners, so that one direction is able to move on its own or alternatively, in conjunction with the second direction. There is a visible improvement and an absence of interlocking turning vehicles. Frankly, I am surprised this used to happen at all. The most frequent madness was at Holborn Circus. When conditions are prime, thirty or so cars successfully immobilise themselves, and honestly, I do not understand the reason. It is not unusual for the wisdom of a simple pedestrian to extricate the cars, in lieu of a traffic policeman. This whirligig is fast disappearing, and I trust that with improving road manners, turning traffic will not lock itself into immobility. A more basic solution is No Right Turns.

I have not forgotten an August day when I and another cab driver sorted out a 100 strong car jam on the Sloane Street- Knightsbridge SW 1 junction. No sooner did we clear an opening to free the key vehicles, then all the cars following, tried to fill the space and recreated the identical hold up. No doubt my passenger thought I should have been at the wheel of my taxi, but I might still have been there if I had done nothing.

No matter where in London, whenever I need to make a difficult manoeuvre, I find a path opened for me by another cab driver. Though I am accustomed to this, I frequently enjoy this courtesy. I must point out this generosity does not include the passing on of work to jobless cab drivers. It is my contention that the ordinary motorist would make life just that much easier for himself by providing and receiving precisely the type of treatment I have just described. He could yield and be yielded to, by drivers of the same make of car. Vauxhall should yield for Vauxhall and Rover for Rover and so forth. The drivers have at least the make of car in common, and probably much more. But perhaps the idea is that of a daydreamer…

During our holidays abroad we learned a thing or two about possibilities for variations on the Hackney Carriage Laws. When we visited Brussels on one of our holidays, we found that all the cabs were clearly marked that they were authorised by the municipal authorities. Although the police in London do leave their mark in many places over the taxi, it is not as clear as it might be, and it would probably be in the interest of the drivers to have this indicated more adequately, showing that we are the only legal taxis in the Metropolis, and that we alone are under the direct supervision of the Police. In 2023, this is still not adequately visible for out of town or foreign visitors.

My wife and I travelled to Paris a couple of years back. We were on our way to the Lido Cabaret and we wanted a Cab, we saw one and quite naturally it pulled up 100 yards further down the road. We raced after it, only to be met with a stream of French from the driver. Our pooled French added together was only up to sixth form standard. My wife understood exactly what he was saying without understanding a single sentence. "I am going home but if you are going my way, I will be happy to take you". The actual words were different but the meaning was crystal. We were lucky and arrived at the Lido Club well on time.

Bumps. Sitting beside the River Seine one sunny Sunday March morning, I was sipping my coffee and dunking my croissant when I heard a bang. I looked up and saw that there had been a triple collision. It was of the bonnet to bumper variety. The state of the cars drew my attention, as I realised that they were already all scratched and dented in any case. As the 3 drivers went to assess the damage, I noticed that most of the passing cars, were battle scarred, bore scratches and minor dents and were also much dirtier than their London counterparts. Meanwhile, the owner of the lead car, with a Gallic shrug of the shoulders, entered his car and drove off. The remaining two drivers, philosophically dismissed the new marks to their cars smiled and departed, without bothering to exchange particulars. I mentally applauded. After all what are bumper bars for, if not to be bumped?

The British Sunday morning car washing ceremony, a pride prompted fetish, no doubt promulgated by suburban car owners, has invaded and routed most other aspects of motoring. I do not for a moment scorn 'Pride in Appearance'. But I have only this week stated my opinion in conversation, that for me a vehicle, is simply a means of 'getting there'.

While serving in BAOR during my National Service, the General commanding our division in Germany, came to inspect our 20-ton Sherman tank for the Annual Administration Parade. He took one look at the tank we had been working on for weeks, and informed our Colonel that it was not a toy but a weapon of war. The hand painted nuts and bolts the glistening hand grips were there to be used and not to be idolised. I endorse his remark not only in its original context, but also in relation to privately owned cars. I am fully aware that scratches and dents detract from the value of a vehicle. I also know that a dirty vehicle seems to show a lazy owner, or perhaps one who spends his time more profitably. But a car is not a toy. It is simply a means of moving from place to place. The worship of car wax is yet again materialism, driving society in its image. Because of this, the means of transport becomes a statement of status. As such, the car is sacred, not to be bumped, scratched or dented. Mind my bumper please!

Pedestrians are no different from drivers when it comes to crossing a street. For example, around London's Piccadilly Circus, there are 3'6" high unbroken barriers to usher those on foot to the three traffic light controlled pedestrian crossings. The lights are there for the sole reason of conducting walkers safely through the circling traffic, yet there are always those who instinctively, defy the red lights in front of them or clamber over the fences. No action is taken against these people, though jay walking is an offence. It follows the premise 'If He can do it so can I'. Traffic lights earn their own respect – except by the most foolhardy. The lights exist to protect life. They are there to be obeyed.

Chapter 16
Tours, Ceremonies, and Embassies

The most difficult days to work are 'State Occasions'. Roads have to be closed and bedlam overtakes chaos. The re-routing of traffic because of closed roads, shunting buses and cabs into alternative streets is tedious but inevitable, frustrating, but necessary if London is to keep its tourist attractions. Thousands of workers and shoppers, find themselves infuriated in order that a potentate can pass by in seconds, and then London traffic is allowed to return to its daily routine. The City of London has conceded, and Lord Mayor's Parades are on Weekends. Should the opening of Parliament, Kings and Presidents making State Visits come on a weekend? Half the essence of these occasions is spectator participation.

In the 1960s there were no mobile phones, or instant messaging like we have today, in the 21st century. In those days, I only had to keep my eyes open to become aware of what was happening worldwide, and how it was reflected on the streets of London. The quick observation of the number of police officers outside a specific embassy was a clue. Rarely, but occasionally, police forces were massed to prevent a riot, but the solitary constable standing outside the entrance is normally sufficient protection. He often melds into the architecture of the building. Because of his immobility he might be mistaken for a figure from Madame Tussauds.

Some Diplomatic Premises are provided with sentinel type police officers' presence in their doorways, some of these for 24 hours daily. Usually, it is merely a diplomatic courtesy. Over the years the radio and press made a great fuss of demonstrators outside the US Embassy in Grosvenor Square W1. Normally one or two policemen strolling in front of the building, aiding passersby is the standard.

At the Greek Embassy, before it moved to Holland Park W11, a couple of doors away from the US Embassy, a sole copper acts the part of Horatius against the Etruscan hoards. The doorway is so narrow one can imagine the heroic defence of Rome. When protestors were fasting to prevent an execution in Athens, a second policeman made the area more secure. In fact, there is a Mews in a slight depression which the US and Greek embassies shared, which was used to park coach loads of police out of public view. Looking at Saarinen's great Embassy, I frequently wonder whether the sloping ramps which surround it, with their gilded fence, were deliberately designed to withstand mass intruders. Both the US and the Greek embassies are long gone.

Grosvenor Square also boasts The Canadian High Commission and the Indonesian Embassy, neither of which merits the attention of the metropolitan police. But a quarter a mile away in South Audley Street at the Egyptian Embassy, there is a regular police watchman. When things are quiet in the Middle East, he often permitted to stroll 25 yards or so away from the entrance. On a bad day he does not budge. Mayfair boasts many more consulates and embassies, Italy is comfortably housed at the end of a cul-de-sac. Brazil Cuba, and Monaco are not far away.

A second neighbourhood favoured by embassies is Belgravia SW 1 Belgrave Square is favourite with the Norwegian, German, Portuguese, Kuwait, Turkish embassies and the Ghanaian High Commission. Two boast police protecting, the Spanish and the Irish. Such are the magnificent proportions of this grandly designed square that the policemen are scarcely visible. They are part of the scenery.

Rhodesia House on the Strand WC2 has a duty constable during office hours, and then he returns to Charing Cross police station at the end of the day. Should there be a demonstration, then the number of police is increased. I have sometimes wondered if the police force rents out uniforms for consular staff in times of stress. I see these policemen as models on a barometer, who pop up according to the air pressure. One copper normal, two, changeable weather forecast.

Ambassador's residences do not usually qualify in the barometric register. Though not long ago the South African Ambassador's residence at High Veldt in Kensington earned itself a guard, after a disturbance at the Embassy. Quite a few diplomatic residences are cloistered inside Millionaire's Row in Kensington Palace Gardens W8. They sit alongside the next batch of Embassies, Russian, Israeli, Philippines, Czechoslovakia. Each of these has in the event of a crisis a first line of defence: the entrance to this private road. When both gates are open all is normal, but when only one side of the iron gates is open, something is amiss. The duty policemen outside the Russian Embassy are most fortunate, as they are housed in a roofed and glassed hut, in which it is also possible to sit. Of the 'Big Four', France, is the only one with an unguarded building, although there was a watch during the Paris Student Riots of yesteryear. The British Embassy? Well at least one London Cab Driver has been asked for it. Even if he only drove to the Home Office.

At this stage of my life, I find that going out in London is less exhilarating than it used to be, for there are few streets I have not traversed, and there are few sights I have not seen. There is however, the wonderful compensation of being able to, move from place to place without having to resort to reference books. This was particularly helpful, when I was planning to buy a house in 1964. I can assess a street without going there, for a picture springs to mind. Being here, there and everywhere, I am able to sense the feeling of improving or deteriorating neighbourhoods. There are some signs which attracted me. An exterior wall painted white and a pair of coach lights on either side of the front door signal that property prices are rising. I only wish I had the prescience to know where this will happen next.

'Palace' is a magic word to some people, and when someone asks me for 'The Palace' I am often caught out. Two obvious solutions are Buckingham Palace and the Palace Theatre. It might also be a personage asking, so a little politesse is needed to sort out which of the two is required. American tourists enamoured with the word, ask me for the Royal Victoria Palace inadvertently changing the status of the theatre.

Day after day throughout the summer I see it, and day after day I never fail to be impressed. "What's going on today?" ask my riders as I drive round the white marble Victoria Memorial in front of Buckingham Palace. This is no longer possible today (traffic flow has been change for a more suitable system easing both traffic movement while tourists can cross the road in comparative safety).

Half of my passengers answer themselves after asking "What is going on?" "It's only the Changing of the Guards – what a lot of people – it surely can't be like this every day?" It is, and the country's foreign exchange balance benefits greatly. Businessmen consult their watches,

131

smother curses and look back at the crowd again, in amazement. There are hundreds crushed against the high black railings. Railings capped with gold painted points and orbs, with children hanging halfway to the top. No one seems to care about them catching their heads between the bars. A second crowd, draped over the steps and balustrades of the memorial, has a superior vantage point even though it is further from the Palace itself. Sightseers trying to reach that secure eyrie, clear of the maelstrom of circling traffic run foul of the already delayed motorists. It is only when the police lend a hand, that crossing to and from the memorial is not a major hazard. Think of crossing the Place d'Etoile.

London's architecture may change, cities may become uniform, but this is one part of London that is constant. Here at Buckingham Palace is a ceremony that is not going to be replaced with modernity. The Enfield rifle might be replaced by the FN but nothing else. True, The Guards may have retreated behind the railings, finally defeated by intrepid tourists attempting to be photographed together with a Guardsman. There were others who deliberately tried to provoke the duty sentry into making an unplanned movement. The annual increase in tourists is matched by an increased police presence. There are motorcycle police and police inspectors, park police and women police, and of course police on horseback to keep the crowds controlled. They too, even though in uniform, and on duty, add to the festive atmosphere.

A must, for many tourists is to take a selfie with the Household Cavalry cantering along The Mall in the background.

From 11:00 onwards, the coaches begin to pour in; they have passed by Westminster Abbey and the Houses of Parliament, the coach has come from Whitehall via Admiralty Arch, to start the drive down the processional route of The Mall. The passengers, their heads twisting in concert, react to their guides' commentaries. Winston Churchill statue stands in Parliament Square, and James Cooke of Australasia fame is ever present in The Mall. Suddenly, out of the blue, Busboys brushed, rifles spotless, shoes glistening in the sun, the next, or relief duty unit marches in front of the coach on its way to the Palace. A mounted policeman waves the coach on, and it overtakes the troops pressing forward into the now dense mass of sightseers, spilling off the wide pavements into the road. Probably no one has noticed the birds' nests in the sails of the model ships topping the double gas lights. In the summer, these ornaments are frequently hidden by the foliage of the parks' trees. Sometimes the coach holds up traffic as it disgorges its load of leisurely trippers.

There are coaches arriving from foreign countries, joining the ever-loyal British holiday makers. After they have set down their loads of visitors at the foot of Constitution Hill, they drive to park in line together with the other coaches, nose to tail. On a normal summer's day there could be about 40 coaches. On a sunny day they will stand, with their sunroofs open to the sky, letting in the cool air. A brief breathing break for the drivers before they have to recommence battle with London's traffic.

Inside the coaches, the drivers sit quietly smoking, and occasionally they will be able to enjoy a conversation with a tour guide, who for some reason, has not accompanied his group. Opposite, on the other side of the road, the chauffeurs in black and grey suits stand alongside their glittering limousines and chatter in the sun, their peaked hats and gloves rest idly on the drivers' seat. I have noticed quite a few guides amusing themselves by walking through the crush with their umbrellas held upwards at arms' length. The handle of the brolly makes a rallying point for a particular group when the brolly is upside down.

Now and again, I am required to drive round our metropolis showing the major points of interest. If the riders come from the north of the country, they strike a hard bargain, and do not intend to actually visit the sites. United States visitors often want to know the age of a building and what if any, connection with royalty. I have attempted to describe the sights in French and in Dutch, but it is very difficult for me, as I truly do not know too much about the sites, even in English. I frequently try to put myself in place of the passenger and endeavour to see London as he does. If they are total strangers, every turn, every set of traffic lights, gives them a new aspect to absorb and place in their memories. As they see Oxford Street's famed premises John Lewis, Selfridges, Marks and Spencer's, and HMV, they are most likely unconsciously assessing it, and comparing it to the equivalent buildings back home.

At night, the display of neon lights is perhaps rated 'as good as' or 'better than', Times Square, Champs Elysée. Maybe the Embankment is compared to the Lungo Tevere.

Chapter 17
Locals (no, not pubs)

A gentleman whose manners probably deteriorated in ratio to the quantity of drink he swallowed, left a Chelsea Restaurant in Kings Road SW1 in the company of a young lady. She told him the address, giving the district first: Earl's Court SW5 and then added Warwick Gardens. On arrival at Earls Court Road, she denied having ever been there before. The gentleman then reiterated to me Earl's Court, and questioned if I knew where I was driving. I responded saying we had already driven down Earl's Court Road a couple of minutes previously and we would now return. Then I was told to get to the station quickly or it would all be the worse for me. It happens that Earls Court Road Station has two major entrances. Again, they poured their wrath on me, as they had not recognised the Warwick Road, Station entrance. I was now instructed to get to the Earl's Court Road entrance and buck my ideas up. Warwick Gardens is unusual for there is No Entry for vehicles from *both ends*. I suspect she had always entered the road on foot.

Arriving there, they told me to pull up on the left. Face to face out of the cab they called me a clot, then something worse. I asked the young lady if she knew what the man had said. She was disconcerted, for she had thought to impress not to offend. I explained it was disgusting, and how could anyone speak like that. Finally, the fare was paid, and the relationship between the new acquaintances was no longer as smooth as it had been a half hour earlier, but I was too disgruntled to care. A few polite words, and we could have arrived at the precise location without mishap.

It happened at the destination, when a healthy young woman well dressed with restrained behaviour did not move from her place at the back of the cab. I shuffled. She did not move. I stopped the engine. She did not move. I contorted myself in my seat so that I could turn and face her. She smiled the smile of a little girl in trouble. I glared. "Driver" she declared hesitantly "I can't get out the cab". To me she looked well. "Well," I asked, "What seems to be the trouble?".

"I have dropped my gloves and I can't pick them up….". In my mind I substituted *"Won't pick them up* for *Can't pick them up"*. The little girl smile changed to an earnest woman's smile. I opened her door and picked the gloves up. She smiled in gratitude, and I moved aside to let her out.

"Thank you so much driver – I am superstitious you see" she uttered in an explanatory comment. I praised the fates and drove off.

Experience teaches. When I started work, I did not understand too much of what went on. I am still embarrassed at my behaviour when a contented young couple laughed their way home to Hackney. Somehow, their youth and the friendly atmosphere, penetrated my lonely place at the steering wheel. On arriving, perhaps a little too self-righteously, perhaps a little too beneficently I declared," Never mind the 7/6d on the meter just give me 5/-, that's what I have to pay my boss". They looked at one another, at a loss to understand what had happened. Suddenly they understood; the girl blushed and turned away. The boy became embarrassed and could not cope. I had made a gaff, but with the very best intentions. The couple were handsome, and were in a happy mood, and as I mentioned it had its effect on me. When I picked them up in the West End and when they exited the cab, I had seen the girl pretty though she was, had a badly crippled leg which made walking very difficult. On the way I had decided to reduce the meter fare so I should gain nothing from it. I simply wanted the lad to repeat his evening out with her without being skint. I said none of this of course, but the situation was calamitous. There was no remedy. I took the money, thankful for the dark, to hide my embarrassment and drove away.

Tact is needed for another type of person, and that is for those who are coping with a disability, physical or otherwise. This is part of the rationale I must use when I do not spring from my seat to aid someone who is trying laboriously to clamber into my vehicle. The moment I am asked, I will move into action to help. I have learned from experience that people prefer to move under their own aegis rather than be assisted.

The rain was falling heavily the night I was asked for the Victoria Air Terminal. There are three within a short distance of one another, I queried which was required. BOAC, BUA, or Skyways. British Overseas Airways Corporation exists today and was the original state-owned airline created in 1939 until 1974 when it merged with other airlines. Next there is Freddy Laker's British United 1960-70, which finally amalgamated with Caledonian Airways. The last, Skyways, started 1946 terminated 1962. As soon as I saw his ticket, I realised he needed the BEA terminal on Cromwell Road, and he told me that he had made a guess that he needed the Victoria Air Terminal. All's well that ends well. Courtesy on both sides. Problem solved.

When a polite greeting and destination has been given, I respond in a similar vein. A rapport has been created between the passenger and myself. I imagine there is now empathy between us. Arriving at 'point' at Victoria Station, I became involved with a party of young German campers whom I drove to London's sole camping site. They were a party of four and it must have been the peak camping season. They arranged all their bundles neatly into the interior, the luggage compartment, and boot of the taxi and off we set. They were in fine fettle, and I used one or two German phrases I knew.

They were a little put out by the distance we were travelling, and indeed it seemed to me that we were way out of tourist London. Arriving there, in the deep South of London, I saw the not so friendly narrow entry onto the camping site. They checked in, only to find the only place that was free was very close to the site entrance. We were at Crystal Palace SE19 designed by Paxton for the Great Exhibition. Burned down in 1936, it has been a National Sports Centre, and was in the 1960s a camping site, though a couple of Football Cup Finals had once been played there.

We were all astonished at the tiny area they were allotted, and they too were worried. The perimeter they were given to deposit and pitch their gear, was smack bang right up to the next tent. A glance all around showed their site was no different from anyone else's. I helped them unload and wished them a pleasant stay in London in their cramped pitch. They will have to make quite a journey to visit the tourist sites of London. 2022 shows that there is not just a camping site there today, but also a caravan park. It in addition maintains four swimming pools.

I have to try and understand many non-English accents, I do not consider this a trial but more of a challenge. Some of the English accents are greatly amusing. 'O' to 'U' is acceptable, but I still find it funny to hear Brompton pronounced 'Brumton' and Conduit changed into 'Cunduit'.

Harrod's is enunciated by the best people as 'Herod's' for those who are living 2,000 years too late.

Paddington becomes 'Piddington'. One delightful conversion is Pall Mall to 'Pell Mel'. Hence "The Royal Otomobile Clob, Pell Mell driver." I learned early to pronounce Beauchamp Place as 'Beecham Place', but I did not have the heart to react to an American who gave the street the full French title Beau Champ Place. It surely could not have been the same day when a fare asked for the 'Aliens Hall'. I kind of guessed he was referring to the Aeolian Hall. I thought I had heard every variation of John Lewis until I heard Chong Louis. A destination given to me as 'Flachman' became a riddle, until I realised the speaker was Spanish and then it became Flaxman, which is the telephone exchange code, for Chelsea. I then knew to drive to SW1, and we were started on our search.

I am not impressed by the affluent, artisan or not, who know my name before they have spoken to me. "John" comes top of the list then "Jim" or "Jack". Sometimes, he acknowledges my status with "Chief", "Governor", occasionally shortened to "Guv" or "Boss". There is another form of address which acknowledges we are both members of the proletariat with "Mate" "Cock" or "Pal".

Early one morning, my fare, after we had exchanged pleasantries, weather, traffic, etc. asked me "Are you sure you are a cab driver?". I thought for a while, and then declared that I was. After all, I have been driving a taxi for the last six years, and I had a large green badge covering my heart. "You do not have a cockney accent", recriminatingly. I apologised and said that my 'posh' accent was only an affectation. "But you call your passengers 'Sir' don't you?" I was delighted and scored my first point. "The correct phrase is "'Guv', Guv". "I think you used to read Law and turned it in". This comment to console himself. I disillusioned him once more, "My education finished at 16". However, to cheer him up I told him my most humorous form of address "'Guv' Sir". He perked up a little at this, and related that he had only recently returned from the States, and was horrified as to what has been happening in the Social Strata of yesteryear. "Your accent has disturbed me and I shall spend the rest of the morning utterly upset". As I set down, in order to calm my passenger, I asked for "'arf a crahn Guv" and pretended to fumble for change in a non-existent waistcoat. He responded with a friendly grin.

That day, an energetic woman sprang frantically into the cab and asked for "Hornton Street please, and will you drive as fast as you can!". The appeal had no effect on me for we were in Oxford Street during the lunch hour, and the traffic was only moving in fits and starts. "Overstayed your lunch?" I asked when the lights turned red. "Oh no, nothing like that, I am going to a fire!". Was she a pyromaniac, could fire be the…… "Fire?" I murmured when we stopped at the next red light. "Yes, in my flat…" she responded. Electric fire? Fire in the flat? How did she know? "How do you know?". We had progressed four blocks,
"I left two eggs cooking on the stove three hours ago".

At last, we cleared Marble Arch, and I decided that maybe the matter was urgent and began to speed. I had visions of fire appliances, frantic neighbours, police, water and bedlam. I drove faster and Bayswater merged into Notting Hill.

"What was the saucepan made of?"
"Aluminium, that would melt, wouldn't it?"
"No…" the rest of the answer was lost in the roar of my taxi engine.

Finally, I careered round the last corner in a manner that made my heart sing. We turned into Hornton Street W8. No appliances. No crowds gazing upwards. Perhaps it was over. A sigh of relief from over my shoulder. "There is no smoke coming from my window, I think it is all right. Here you are driver and thank you".

Initially, I was furious when a fare sat down in the rear of the cab and started checking each street as we drove down it. Yes, he was using a street map. I interpreted this to be a passenger who implicitly queried the route, but gradually it became clearer to me that the fare was finding his way around a new neighbourhood.

Similarly, the punters who say as soon as they have given me the address "Is it far"? leave me in a quandary, if I say Yes, it is possible the person will walk off. If I say No, the punter will then think I am taking him for a ride. The correct answer is another question "How long is a piece of string?". The direct question easily answered is, "How far is it?" This can be answered by time, distance, or price.

I have become, as must most cab drivers, a cynic with a stoic attitude, as I am in service to the London population that are able to pay me for my driving service. I see the population in all their moods. Drunk or sober, on business, in a hurry, late for the train, out with the boys, and joyously flirting with a partner. Personalities change as fast as the traffic lights. I earn my living driving, and am obliged to take on all comers, both my passengers and other road users. I do so daily, and with more than average luck, win!

Chapter 18
London by Night and In The Rain

The Mansion House is the venue for many Livery Companies, when they hold their periodic banquets. There are today more than 100 of them, but the original 12 have a special place in the hierarchy. They acquired the title Worshipful Company, for they associated themselves with a specific Saint or Church. The word *livery* relates to their distinctive clothing. One night it might be the Worshipful Company of Spectacle Makers, the Turners, or perhaps the Company of Carmen. Many of the original companies still maintain their City premises. Trapping, one night when the members were leaving an event, I started to chat with a lone rider, a member of the Carmen's Society. He explained, while talking of the traditions, that originally, they did not use motorised vehicles, and nowadays there are very few old-fashioned road hauliers who use horse drawn vehicles in their work, but carmen today, are mainly proprietors of motorised vehicles. They are entitled as of old, to certain privileges such as leaving their vehicles in appointed spots, even if they are in the middle of a parking meter zone. They may also, without risk of prosecution, cool the wheels of their vehicles or axles of the vehicles in which they have been travelling, in the manner used by Carmen throughout the ages. A discreet activity, best unseen by the public. In private, I must admit to using this privilege even though I am not a member of the Company.

When I did the Knowledge, and it was of course in daytime. It was a delight to discover the Apothecaries Hall, the Tallow Chandlers Hall, Fishmongers Hall and indeed the Salters Hall, Glassmakers Hall and many others. There was and is still, a hidden dignity in the history of these anachronisms that sustain a calm contrast to the crude bustle of pedestrians and buses, jostling daily in the narrow streets of the City of London.

NIGHT: The dearth of traffic at night makes driving simpler, and journey time is cut down considerably. Empty roads allow one to approach an average 30 mph compared to the 10 mph of the daytime (in 2024 TomTom recorded in the Independent Newspaper that a 6-mile journey in London, is the slowest city in which to drive to drive in the world!). Higher speeds allow the cab driver to cover more ground in the constant search for the next punter. On the other hand, recrossing the deserted City of London after an East End job adds many more 'dead miles', without a chance of seeing a waiting person on the curb. A set down at Liverpool Street Station has the same disadvantage. Some winter months throw up a banquet or two at a City Livery Company. Additionally, there are occasional events at the London's Guildhall.

On these winter nights everything is topsy turvy, the tables are turned, and it is the streets which are quieted. The activity is taking place at the Livery Halls with polished cars, well dressed men, and women laughing and conversing as they arrive and depart the event. I am always contented to rank outside of these Trades Halls, with their historic splendour. The old-fashioned buildings boasting their architectural design, is reason enough for me to sit there waiting, with the occasional reward of an inwards glance at the old fashioned chandeliers and paintings adorning the walls. Some of the lonely waiting times becomes magical.

Not so many nights ago I was turning the cab around in a rather restricted mews in West London, when I needed to utilise that extra foot or so into someone's garage. To my astonishment, I found myself inside a garage which was a small art gallery. The hanging artwork was illuminated, and displayed as if this was the norm. Perhaps it is.

For me, the most impressive, is the Caledonian Ball, where elegant females clothed in full length evening dress with tartan decorations are escorted by their consorts in kilts and dinner jackets. This takes place in Park Lane's Grosvenor Room, which is London's largest Ballroom. Equally splendid but somewhat different, is the gigantic Festival Hall decorated with a myriad of balloons and with masses of jolly students in fantastic costumes, dancing through the night hours celebrating their university graduations. A once in a lifetime event. A step forwards for them in life's progress.

Not mentioned so far is the annual Chelsea Arts Ball with its collection of artistic socialites in exotic fancy dress. Celebration of the New Year here, decrees decorum and the humdrum are left behind, and artistic fervour takes over. It was sadly cancelled for a couple of years during the COVID pandemic.

Very little of London remains active into the wee, small hours. Newspapers once printed here for all over the nation are now printed locally for limited areas. True, fresh food markets are alive. Lone buses traverse their routes while underground trains flit into and out of lonely stations. Keeping the City warm, are the suburbs, built in a circle all around on both sides of the river Thames. These too are dead areas at night; the residents go to sleep early, and only become alive with the dawn hours, as the first early commuters leave for the next day's work. They are followed by the daily masses that surge inwards to repopulate the City and Business centres, all building the new day's pulsating economic hub. The fresh food Markets have nearly completed a night's work e.g., Billingsgate Fish Market has catered for the morrow's needs. The City continues to enjoy enjoys its nightly rest.

In the East by vibrant Whitechapel is still dormant and Westwards Fleet Street is putting the presses to rest. To the South, giant warehouses stand empty and dead (1960s). During the 'dead' hours the traffic lights rarely change, there is insufficient traffic for them to control. It is only in the West End night spots, where the lights are finally being turned off. Meanwhile, Smithfield's meat market supplies, are making their way to the shops and the myriad of London Hotels and Restaurants.

Covent Garden has provided the fruit and vegetables for thousands. London is now awake and at work, suburbia is active, involved within itself. The City, once more engages the world in commerce. On one small bend by the river, Parliament will soon involve itself in the interests of the nation.

One warm summer night I was approached by a group of young flighty things in full evening dress, accompanied by tuxedoed men, and asked to drive to Covent Garden. My imagination took an immense leap, and I saw them entering into the Market bending down and beginning to shift crates around. On the other hand, there are a number of bohemian types who utilise the Market for their own delectation. They want to experience the thrill of an all-night coffee stall used by the market men who need a break.

I have seen young would-be debutantes prancing around in bare feet amongst the filth, discarded vegetables, and broken containers. I imagine that they think to themselves that they are really experiencing life, and must now surely be recognised among the cognoscenti as true Bohemians. This is how some of the newest generation lust after an exciting life. I doubt this is happening in 21st century, Nine Elms, New Covent Garden Fruit Vegetable and Flower Market, which by the way is the largest in the UK is in fact open and welcomes visitors, even dilettantes.

Well before midnight not far from Old Compton Street, a fellow whispered to me in a conspiratorial way "The Roman Room" and winked. I was delighted to at last be introduced and be included amongst those who knew. He explained it was not the Roman Room in Knightsbridge *or* the 'Sala Romana', but that it was in Soho, and that he did not have the address. We penetrated into deepest Soho and started our enquiries by asking likely looking characters and other drivers, who all knew of exotic places to visit, but none knew of the Roman Room.

In the end, my fare recalled he had a phone number in his little black book, and he left the cab to enter the first phone box and find the address. When he returned, he told me it was 'Raymond's Revue Bar' – rarely have I been so disappointed. 2023 has it recorded as permanently closed, so do not ask your driver to take you there.

There was a period when the Police conceived the idea of push bike patrols. They might have been old fashioned, but they were not only fast and unhindered in their progress, but silent as well. As anyone who cycles will tell you, the bike is the fastest way through stationary traffic, and perhaps the lack of the blue light and siren would not alert any wrongdoers in advance. This was in the days before gallons of paint had been spread alongside road gutters by the authorities, and parking meters were just a dream source of income for the boroughs. Stop Press 22nd August 2023, the police are back on push bikes again after 60 years, this time to catch mobile phone snatchers.

Using bicycles to get through Soho's crowded streets worked for a while, but slowly became a liability. It is conceivable that the moment the copper dismounted and left his bike, it was nicked by the next wrongdoer.

There was and is, a regular job for cab drivers which arises from the parking congestion and its fellow, obstruction. The work was and still is of course, to drive to car pounds, where illegally parked vehicles have been taken. The dismayed passengers rarely give a good tip, knowing they would have to pay a fine for the parking offence to retrieve their car. Arriving at the car pound one night with an irate passenger, I saw a *Hot Dog Stand* probably towed away while the vendor's back was turned. It was standing waiting forlornly in a lonely corner for someone to empty its now cold, and greasy hot dogs!

Cafe proprietors in all areas were becoming bored with the towing or carrying away of vehicles. The regularity of their own vehicles parked outside their own premises being lifted on the back of a lorry and then driven far way, began to spoil the novelty. First time visitors to these areas were dismayed at the experience, and the shock of not finding their cars, gave rise to an immediate fear that their transport had been stolen. The removal of cars also happened in the Knightsbridge areas – especially around 'Herods', where again and again drivers told me that they had been parking in that particular spot for years and nothing had happened. An explanation was too difficult, so usually I shut up and one could only commiserate with first time visitors to London.

"Would you take me please..." When a beautiful woman asks me this, I am worried, to say the least. I suppose every male driver will react differently, but each one would surely be on his mettle. Drivers would quickly estimate the feasible routes to Chelsea or wherever, the shortest and quickest route with least traffic, and then, attempt to while away the journey with friendly banter to pass the time more pleasantly.

"Driver" and then a winsome pause, "Will you do me a favour?"
"Certainly Miss, if I am able."

The favours are varied but never involve personal contact. Young women are a rule unto themselves. Men too, vary. Some females do not speak, some do not smile, others suggestively slide their hand over yours as they pay the fare. Some chatter, some close the dividing window. All seem to be in a hurry, and out of breath, in a fluster- late for work or for a date. "Do you have the time driver?". "Yes miss, it is seven o'clock - is that too late or too early?". "Oh, driver that is terrible, I have to be there at six forty-five". I wonder at the anguished gasp, is it of satisfaction or dismay. I am never sure.

Moods and acumen play a part of working the streets of modern London. I had just driven past a pair of unlikely riders: a pair of youngsters in short trousers, tousled hair, and knitted sweaters. They did not seem to be worthy of my attention as they were just kids. Something made me do a U-turn, and though they did not hail me this time I stopped alongside them. They approached the cab and asked the fare to Liverpool Street. I guessed it to be between four and five shillings. Disappointed and disconcerted they declined at that price. However, I decided to drive them there with no payment, as I could not see them walking the four or five miles without incident. Someone else walking home heard the conversation, and hearing the philanthropy, thought he too would cash in on the offer, but I told him no. Then during the drive to Liverpool Street, I found out that these two youngsters had been engine spotting and had lost track of time. They had recorded a great collection of numbers and were not in the least put out by the time of day, and were enjoying every minute of the taxi ride. I left them with the injunction not to talk to any strangers, even though I knew these words would not mean a thing to this pair. It made me quite worried, but they remained as happy as sandboys. I hoped that when they were on familiar ground in Liverpool St. Station that they would be safe. I trusted they would go straight home.

RAIN: When the combined whirr of the wiper motor and click of the windscreen wiper's blades repetitiously bear too deep into my senses, I begin to associate the globules of rain on the screen with beads of sweat about to form on my brow. Rational thinking becomes numb, as I wait for the wet to transfer from the front window to my face. The *click, click*, as the wiper blade meets the window frame, the judder and click as it then rides back up over the ledge, irritates. *Click. Click.*

Without notification, the traffic of which I am a part, is now reducing speed for a variety of reasons, including the possibility of a skid as they stop or slow down. But also, pedestrians are likely to pelt across the road to avoid a soaking. *Whirr-Whirr*. More congestion. *Click-Whirr*.

There is a second fortunate side to the rainfall, and that is the sudden demand for taxis. People who otherwise would have been happy to walk to their next destination, now call and signal frantically for any passing taxi to pick them up. The illusion that traffic density has suddenly increased, is upsetting but it is symptomatic of our London road system. It can be simply that there could have been a heavy shower somewhere, or even worse, a local flood. There is potential for a local traffic hold up, which in turn, causes more holds up for following traffic. Blast it, the residue rubber left from the tyres on the road has been thrown up with the splashes of preceding cars, and it is beginning to make my windscreen greasy and difficult to see through. Maybe the blade is now covered in a black film of greasy rubber.

Sitting at the steering wheel, I feel I am an integral part of a community constantly moving en mass around the London road network. We are just like ants in the grass, rushing hither and thither. The rain makes the movements more obvious, people on foot speed up their pace to keep dry.

I use tyres, and pedestrians because they use their feet to propel themselves could be treated as second class, as a minor mini species. This line of thought is of course wrong – all wrong. The more the rain, the more the pedestrian should be given priority, additionally, I must avoid ploughing through puddles and splashing walkers on the pavements. I am sure that there is a school of drivers that say to themselves, *Whoopee, now I can make a great splash. Watch me!* and push their foot hard on the accelerator. The more rain, the more precedence must be given to individuals escaping a rainy dousing. Ultimately, the moment I step out of the cab, I become a pedestrian too. Driving is one world, walking in traffic, another. Perhaps half of the pleasure of walking in the countryside is the absence of cars, enraging the farmer's bull is nothing to blithely ignoring the London Omnibus bearing down on you.

Several times each day, a rapid conscious decision is called for: name it 'The Point of No Return' at which I and every driver, is called upon to instantly react. A sudden change in the traffic lights ahead, the red traffic light appearing abruptly while approaching it at a fair speed. As at all times when driving, there are several factors involved. Primarily most important, danger to pedestrians, then vehicles, in front, behind, and sideways. My vehicle speed is relevant, as are the brakes. Are they sufficiently trimmed to stop the vehicle on the spot? Will the driver 'nose to tail behind me' be able to stop? The time involved in making what could be a crucial decision is negligible. On a major artery, perhaps an exit route from London like the Great West Road, one can legally approach traffic lights at a speed of up to 30 or 40 mph. A decision has to be made. Usually, the cars second and third in line, see the lights at the same time as I, and nothing untoward occurs.

Chapter 19
Villiers Street WC2 and Other Ranks

Each driver has his or her favourite rank. Sometimes, because they turn up good jobs. One of mine is at the foot of Villiers Street adjacent to Embankment Underground Station, and during the late evening when people are still moving around, I often put on the rank there. It appears to me that the jetsam of London is flowing down the slope. The variety and quantity of characters compose a spectrum of contemporary society in 1963. The station continues to serve those still entering London at this night time hour, and at the same time swallows those that have had their fill of entertainment, or have worked their long day sustaining the metropolis. In addition to the homeward bound travellers, are the tramps and homeless who have no distant destination but the nearby all-night coffee stalls. There is an attraction to these stalls, maybe it is the owners, maybe the food, maybe the feeling of bonhomie alongside 'Old Father Thames'. The near fixture is the female newspaper vendor standing in the shelter of the station, who rasps spasmodically "E'En Stann". She continues her croaking for hours, without moving the long-ago smoked cigarette from between her lips.

Laughing and jostling their way down the slope of Villiers Street hill come the duffle coated dudes, the mascaraed molls, with their make up the worse for wear. Now a few bearded beatniks, and the Johnnies in jeans. The numbers of genuine travellers are now diminished. The layabouts at the station entrance eye and mentally undress each chick as she passes; they have nothing more to do, and perhaps have no extra money for one more drink. Soon the flower lady begins to assemble her unsold wares, and her stall is packed up. There is no one else passing by who will take a bunch of roses home. The fruit stall follows suit, having sold out of roast chestnuts earlier in the evening.

Now a couple stroll up to my cab, not to travel, but to ask if there is a cheap hotel nearby which can be reached on foot. The girl complains to her pal, "You can't be much if you won't take a cab". Still the stream of humanity continues on its way downwards towards me, at the foot of the hill. Next, come a group of girls with painted faces who have recently left the Lyceum Dance Hall at the end of the Strand. To add to the excitement, a Catholic Speaker is putting forth his opinions, and once a minute, yet another passer-by informs him "You are a sick in the head ****!".

It was a regular Saturday night when I saw a couple of lads munching hot dogs with total relish, when their eyes fell upon a pair of girls standing, perhaps waiting, under an umbrella. The lads strolled up to the girls and offered them a bite of their hot-dogs. The reply must have been scornful in the extreme, for the males turned purple and had trouble swallowing the rest. The boys stalked off and the girls remained in place giggling for quite a while.

I sit there, and looking upwards follow the hands pacing one another, round Big Benzine, under the floodlit facade of Shellmex House. I unconsciously listen, as many travellers appear to test the acoustics of the station booking area by whistling.

I am writing of only one aspect, a night time one. But it shows a microcosm of today's youth endeavouring to enjoy themselves after a long day or week. It was for me then, a feast of characters dressed up for the night out, ready to spend, to laugh, to drink and have fun. Comprehensive all night underground transport had not yet started.

Just metres away round the corner from the station, besides the all-night coffee stall adjacent to Embankment Underground entrance, there is another set of characters scattered around a competing 'all-night London eatery'. During the day, the stalls catch passers-by, but at night there are regulars, men who seem to drift from stall to stall, persons who seem to rarely comb their hair or indeed have it cut. Their clothes match their hair style, and I would say that they are individuals who find conforming to norms of society difficult.

The stalls are in some way regular haunts, that are occasionally used to receive letters, addressed perhaps to "Sam, The all-night coffee stall, The Embankment. London". I sometimes joined the coterie, standing away from the counter, sipping my drink. It was possible to hear many of their life details as they engaged in conversation.

One Wednesday, my attention was drawn to a pair of hands breaking up dog ends, and using the combined tobacco residues to build a whole cigarette. The manipulator of these fags was explaining how he was to go on holiday. From what to where? I was not close enough to hear the entire story, as the group had drifted away from the stall and had gathered round the warmth of a brazier (a road menders fire). I considered the limitless possibilities of this character's holidays.

Occasionally, I use the rank during the day. There is a handy cafe to buy tea and a cake or a sandwich. I sometimes digest these while waiting for a job. The daytime passers by, are regular office workers, and others come into London to have a day out. Villiers Street rank has helped complete my education of what it means to be a Londoner.

Like every driver, when the time has come to find a rank, I simply locate myself to the nearest. Sitting on a rank in the dark, closeted in the drivers compartment physically separated from the passing world, a feeling of isolation begins to creep in and keep me company. During the night hours, different ranks somehow produce different moods.

Waiting on the rank outside a West End hotel on a chill February night, feeling more and more sorry for myself, as the guests strolled into and out of the well-lit and cosily warm, costly Westbury Hotel, it dawned on me there were three of us in the same predicament. There was the hotel commissionaire, a smartly dressed young woman, and myself. The wind was bitter and there was a touch of rain in the air. There was no doubt about it, all three of us were cold and fed up, as fewer and fewer guests entered the premises. I was the best off of the trio. I was sitting, covered, and could if I had wished, run the engine to keep warm. Every several minutes the commissionaire spun the revolving doors and stepped inside to warm up. I did not believe that the two or three minutes he was indoors, was time enough for the indoor warmth to penetrate his heavy doorman's coat. Nevertheless, he repeated the movement.

The third person in the trio, the girl in the red coat and smart black hat, walked slowly past me again. She was expensively dressed and carried herself with grace. The central fountain maintained a constant splash, as the jets hit the water. The other constant was the noise of the passing traffic on Bond Street, which only changed with the traffic lights. An abrupt surge of cars moving, followed by a pause, while the next group waited for green.

An hotel employee came out to catch a breath of fresh air and chatted with the doorman, both of them eyeing the girl. Neither smirked or grinned, or even gave the young woman a friendly smile. In truth, she was as cold and as bored as they were, as the minutes ticked by. Finally, three guests came out of the hotel door and my hand moved towards the ignition key; luckily, I did not start the cab as out of nowhere a Bentley rolled smoothly into the runway. It now became apparent that there had been a fourth person, who had been sitting and waiting, just like me. Now, "You first" "No, you", until all three guests were neatly ensconced in the vehicle, and the commissionaire had his tip. Still, the girl had no customers, and the wind blew a spiteful icy blast. Some 15 minutes after I had started my vigil, another group exited the hotel, and once again, a car appeared, this time boasting diplomatic CD plates.

After the polite bowing farewells, the two of the party who did not enter the limousine approached me. Hurrah! and I was off, now turning my heater on full blast, after a mere 15-minute wait. Sadly, the doorman and girl remained there exposed to the bitter wind swirling around the cold entrance. Too much wating time to watch events and too little income left me with a rather sour outlook on that dreary night's work.

Chapter 20
Day Work, Lost Property and Moving Jobs

At the moment (1962), in order to create a variety in my work, I work three days and three nights per week. Thus, I am exposed to the gamut of persons who use taxis. I do not join my colleagues who work the airports or the docks. I do not hang around the markets and stations. I enjoy acting on a whim to find my next job, trying to anticipate where work will be. You will only find me on a hotel rank on the rare occasions that there is no cab there before me.

I am well aware of Hotel linkmen who expect a good tip from the cab driver while seating passengers for an 'Airport Job'. This of course, is not fair, as a driver 30 seconds earlier, might well have 'got off for a short ride to Fortnum's'. The unspoken threat is, that in the future, he might call in another taxi – whose driver *will* tip him.

Prices to Heathrow are still queried, and are often irrationally excessive. The earnings on an airport job are greater than on any other journey, as returning from the Airport to Hammersmith is only a 20-minute drive. Fuel cost is negligible, over that 10-mile run. NO real excuse for extra high prices then. There are drivers who work the airport, who have only themselves to blame that minicabs and private hire are booked in advance. Taxi drivers are under no obligation to work there, the metropolis is open to them. If the drivers who rank at airports seem greedy, there is another school of cab drivers who are a credit to themselves and the trade. They transport the blind and disabled at no cost. They help cripples up steps and hoist heavy luggage for the elderly. There are many more of these drivers than the few who besmirch the trade.

It is easy for me to point the cab in the correct direction as soon as I have been given a destination. So, I must be thankful for the Knowledge. Equally, I am primed to have a variety of routes to choose from. I plan ahead to avoid blockages noted when I arrived in the area, thus saving the punter and myself valuable time sitting in a jam. The thinking is not dissimilar to chess: I hold a number of alternatives in my head, and only when I feel my visualised route is suitable, do I make my moves.

Day work has its special passengers. Those who are too tired to continue walking. When I hear "Marble Arch, driver" and it is daytime, and I am travelling from the far end of Oxford Street, my mind begins to boggle. It races along side streets and meets No Entry signs, it leaps at alternative routes and discards them, and finally sinks into a trough of despair, as I realise there is nothing for it but to sit it out and bludgeon my way through Oxford Street with its bustling shoppers. I move steadily as part of a phalanx utilising the entire road space. But knowing the turns off ahead, I drive into the non-turning lane – thus not being held up by a red light on the turning lane. All is not lost.

Harley Street W1 and in its vicinity Wimpole Street, are required by the public daily. There is a mixture of medical consultants and medical facilities in these streets. I make this one of my regular haunts searching for a passenger, as the same people who ride a cab to arrive, will probably need one to depart after visiting a specialist. There are shoppers who need quick and easy transport between stores, sometimes Knightsbridge, otherwise the West End. Local jobs call for skill, for there are many One Ways in these areas, and it is important to know 'side doors' of major businesses. A mistake of forgetting a 'No Right Turn' could double the distance and fare.

A ride from the Dorchester came quickly. I had not waited more than a couple of minutes, and it held me enthralled: Airport or local? Unfortunately, the golden nugget was not for me. It has been, and still is in the purlieu of the regular drivers, who supply the doormen with beer money. So, I got off to Selfridge's. On arrival, we discovered that neither of us had change for the £1 *note*. The fare was 2/-, two bob in old money. My fare offered to nip in and buy a pair of stockings, to obtain change, but was worried she would not find the brand she wanted. So, I decided to pop into the cafe opposite and buy a packet of biscuits. I completed a tour of the self-service counter and returned to my passenger, she paid me and gave me 6d tip for my trouble.

Continuing working, I decided to tour the outer perimeter of the store and see if anyone who was leaving needed me. I drove round to the far side, and who should step out but my lady from the Dorchester. She hailed me, then suddenly noted that it was me again, and lowered her hand and let me pass. She must have gone into the giant store raced across the floor, and this would have been no mean feat, even if it were empty, and then come out at the far side. Why? I wondered. There was not sufficient time for her to have bought anything. Had she forgotten something? I remain puzzled to this day.

Like clockwork, there are people who wait until nearly 15:00 each day, and then rush to enter the bank before closing time. I was totally nonplussed when a middle-aged man entered the cab, and demanded the 'National Bank'. I pulled away from the curb expecting to be told which branch, and then made my usual physical contortion, which could easily dislocate one or other of my shoulder blades, and tried to gain more information. I was informed it was the National Bank, Moorgate. When we did arrive, it turned out to be the National Bank of New Zealand. Was I supposed to have recognised his accent? I tendered the required receipt and drove off. I bet, that many of the riders travelling by cab are on expense accounts, and the company they work for is paying the fare.

It was always a pleasure to watch the crocodile of boys in Knightsbridge, clad in their brownish orange uniform. The Hill House School lads with wonderful mops of hair, doffed their caps in respect to the drivers who have stopped to let them cross the busy roads. Sometimes this occurs twice, once on either side of the central island. The disarray of their locks, increasing with each cheeky gesture.

Sitting in traffic there is much to be observed. To my amusement, one day I noticed a sticker which was attached to a woman driver's car: "Watch my behind not hers". The same day I read on a British Railways goods van "Please clean me good St. Pancras". The epigram was scrawled into the dust and grime on the rear of the vehicle.

While on day work, I sometimes met my wife and we would lunch together in Mayfair where she worked. It sometimes took me 15 minutes to find a parking place on a meter. But one day, after I had seen an elephant standing at a meter and the mahout having a row with the meter man, I decided to leave the cab on an unused cab rank in Berkeley Square. All went well, but sooner rather than later, a meter man having noted he could not fine me, called in the law. So, I was summonsed and fined for not being on duty with the first cab on the rank.

One day when my wife returned to work early, I sat in the rear of the vehicle which was parked at a meter for which I had paid, and read my newspaper. This annoyed a female motorist, and she tried to make the meter attendant move me from my meter. I laughed at them, for if I could not sit on the empty cab rank, then I would take up a space, on the scarce parking meters.

Day and night, people leave articles in the cab. Sometimes it is a religious tract, other times it is spectacles, gloves or even a handbag. Once, a woman who had obviously been presented with some roses several hours previously, left the cab and gave them to me as a tip. As half the petals had already fallen, I placed them respectfully on the curb and drove off. Sometimes a comb slips out of someone's pocket. One day I was too embarrassed to penetrate to the depths of a Mayfair Hair Salon to return a pair of elegant elbow length silk gloves which my fare had left, so I handed them to the receptionist and forewent any gratitude.

The official procedure is to hand the forgotten article in to the nearest police station within three days of finding it. One has to relay the details of the time, place, and perhaps destination, while prominently displaying one's taxi driver badge. This by-law is applicable even on one's day off, even when walking into the local 'nick'. Once this antiquated procedure is completed. The article is sent to the Lost

Property Department of the Public Carriage Office, where it remains for up to three months, or until it is claimed. Unclaimed articles are returned to the driver who found them.

My first find was a pair of gloves. I found that the Duty Officer took ages to complete the recording procedures, and I realised that they were not keen to waste their time with pettifogging procedures. I have since returned various odds and ends. I followed this procedure, until one day, someone who was travelling to Sloane Square left his wallet in the taxi. Luckily, I spotted this before I pulled away. I rushed into the building waving the bulging pigskin article in the air. I ran up a couple of flights of stairs to where the lift had stopped, and rang the bell to the flat that I thought the gentleman had entered. I then enquired if he had left the full wallet in my taxi just a moment ago. "Oh yes, so I did, thank you driver" and immediately shut the door. I was disconcerted, to put it mildly. I made a point of remembering this incident so as not to get caught out a second time.

We are all human. I too sometimes forget things. But the variety of items left behind after a journey is fascinating. This includes dropping and losing a ring in the taxi, or a wristwatch, or a shoe. I thought perhaps it was a stunt, when a present-day would-be Cinderella, tried to make me chase around after her and into the Cafe Royal. For this was where she had gone. Did she really think I would wander into the Cafe, wearing my duffle coat and cap and try the shoe on all the ladies. Surely not! Instead, I gallantly left the shoe with the doorman, described the foot it fitted and left.

More than once, a passenger enters the cab, and directs me to the nearest barbecue or fish and chips shop, and then returns with a parcel wrapped in newspaper. The journey ends with the tasty smell of the meal wafting forwards as I suppress my hunger. I am paid, and then discover that not only has the punter enjoyed his banquet but he has left the trappings - chicken bones or spare chips, for the benefit of the next rider. I did once, in earlier days, drive after the rider and hurl the residue of his meal at him with my blessings.

A Ronson lighter that I handed in to the police was not claimed, and I was able to keep that. I still have it even though I no longer smoke. When one night I discovered a diamond ring in the rear of the taxi, I was ecstatic. What inspired me to look, and how I found it I still do not know, but there were 3 diamonds set in gold, and I put it in my pocket while I considered which was the nearest police station. Spying a milk machine en route, I stopped and bought a carton, and while I was drinking, I thought I would take a second look at the trophy and confirm it was what I had thought. I found a hall mark inside the ring. The only complication was, that it appeared to be in four parts. I twisted the ring in the light of the street lamps, and then to my chagrin, I read 'gilt' (lightly covered in gold leaf), and realised that any wishful thinking was dreams.

So, some months later when I discovered a lady's dress watch in what appeared to be chromium with a paste inset, I knew it was no good and worth nothing to the owner or me. I considered it to be very ordinary, but when it was not claimed I would be able to give it to my wife, and she would be able to wear it with a modicum of distinction. I stopped at a City Police Station and after the usual interrogation, was permitted to enter deeper into the building where the item could be registered. I made my report and thought no more of the matter. To my surprise it was only a few days later that I was instructed to report to the Public Carriage Office to receive a serious reward for returning this platinum and diamond wristwatch. I was told that for the rest of my driving career I would never have a find of this value again.

Once was indeed enough, yet I still have that constant incentive to turn around as each passenger leaves and check that there is nothing left behind. In the 21st century, I listened to a Cab Driver on Television, and he related that telephones are frequently forgotten and that they have a high value. He also explained it was quite simpler to do some of the jiggery pokery that modern persons do, and locate the owner of the article. He vindicated me by commenting it was very time consuming to hand the article in at a police station.

When we were living in Finsbury Park, I finished work at 02:00 on a Saturday night, and while locking up, I found a pair of gloves. Next day, Sunday, we decided to stroll round to the nearest police station, only to be reprimanded for not coming in sooner! On another occasion after we had moved to Woodford, I again finished late and discovered a box of beauty make up. My wife suggested to me that it might be worth £50. When taken to the Police Station and it was itemised, we all realised it had some £200 worth of bits and pieces. We were offered the reward when it was collected, but declined, and let the money stay with the police charity fund.

Alistair Cooke in one of his famous weekly "Letters from America", told us on the radio, in his laconic manner, how he had left his camera in a taxicab while holidaying in London. He maintained that he was not surprised to have the camera returned to him in his hotel within the hour. Good copy for him. Yet, when he returned home to the States, he committed the same forgetfulness, leaving some swathes of cloth, a present for his wife, in the New York Yellow cab. That was the last that he saw of them. He made a complimentary comparison between a London cabby and a New York hack.

Deliveries and Removals

During the day I frequently make deliveries; the articles that I carry are many and diverse. The most usual are coats and dresses for the shmutter trade. These are frequently from the wholesaler to the retailer.

Now and again, I have shoes in their original boxes, though these are not heavy. The rear windows are blocked off by the stacks, and my usual rear view vision while driving, is halved. I was hailed close to Borough Market on a rainy morning, when the scruffy young man with a scarf who stopped me, pointed to a barrow loaded with crates of fruit. There were not many, and the solid wooden barrow did not appear to me to be overloaded. But once the apples, pears, and vegetables were inside the cab, it looked like a farmers' market. The cab, viewed from the street, revealed the rear elliptical springs were almost flat, such was the weight. Not only was it too late to request the guy to unload it, but I understood as we loaded the cab, that he was not a person to be frustrated. I did the job, but drove with the utmost caution, as the road springs would probably have snapped at the slightest bump.

Not too long ago I had to deliver a meal to the fabulously expensive London Clinic, where the cuisine can surely not be bettered. Yet the meal came from the equally expensive Caprice Restaurant. Some patients, it seems, cannot be satisfied. I have driven Rocking Chairs to be photographed at a studio, and have delivered photos, flowers, and even kosher food. I have heard our closed-circuit radio dispatcher tell a driver to collect the house keys of someone who had forgotten to take them to work, and now, the cab driver was required to collect them and then deliver them at the man's workplace. I trust the person who forgot his keys did not forget what work he was supposed to be doing.

In the day times, I, like every one driving and walking in London, is subject to posters and hoardings. All-day drivers are perhaps the most susceptible to their messages. The placards that I find most amusing and interesting are the ones that promote the sale of the evening papers. The Headlines at the newsstands, which alter as I drive round, are replaced as soon as a new batch of papers arrive. Can you remember the song of the news vendors "Star, News, or Standard"? It is just about possible by reading these placards, to keep abreast of unfolding events. No mobile phones in those days. A prime example occurred while I was driving in Grosvenor Square, there I read on an Evening News banner: A MAN HAS BEEN KILLED. By the time I reached Trafalgar Square I found out that he was a LONDONER. Approaching Aldwych, I knew he worked in FLEET STREET. A picture began to form in my mind. Holborn, the headlines told me he was a DEEP SEA DIVER. Glancing at an actual newspaper headline as I waited at traffic lights, I saw he was a CHAMPION DIVER. Someone's newspaper, later in the day, told me he had DROWNED IN AN OCEAN PLUNGE. I did not need to buy an evening paper that day.

Variety is indeed spicy, and every driver can list a series of episodes which are just part of the daily patina of happenings in metropolitan cabbing. A five-year-old actually said to me, "Thank you, my good man". Preposterous.

A Rolls Royce driver explained to me that he drove in traffic, bluffing his route through, "Who would want to collide with a Roller? All I do is put £5,000 worth of machinery in front of you and dare you to damage it!".

Over the last centuries, London taxi drivers are considered to be both "Rogues who grossly overcharge" or "Angels who will go to great lengths to aid a passenger". The first group includes lazy, aggressive, rude men who have acquired a reputation of sometimes overcharging passengers. There appear to be no greys in this matter, either the drivers are great, or they take advantage of foreign visitors and strangers. Sadly (and happily), this is London. A North Country couple related to me that, staying at an hotel when they asked the concierge for tickets for a specific London Show, they were told there were none, but plenty for another show which they did not want to see. North Country sense prevailed, they went to the theatre box-office and discovered that that there were seats available. Myself a Londoner, I too have 'unfortunately' been presented with an inflated bill at a Night Club, when drink could have affected my memory, and once again, in a restaurant, where I was charged for double sized portions which we had not ordered. London is not for the naive.

Driving for these few years, I have learned to be on guard against potential scams, risks, and con artists. Toughened now, a mask of cynicism protects me, and I do realise that there is always more to a situation than meets the eye. Tricksters artfully operate under a mask of calm.

The public in general are not ill intentioned, and I can now give as good as I can take. The work is not dissimilar to a kaleidoscope. There are a set amount of contents which can produce an unlimited series of patterns, yet they are all formed from the same basic elements. The sheer futility of driving round in London often occurs to me. The earth is a planet, perhaps a small one, revolving inside a gigantic universe. I have to reconcile myself that I am driving inside a very limited area day in day out.

Certainly, I am earning a living, clothing and housing my family, but what insignificant ant-like labour is this? Revolving, twisting, cavorting, in this the smallest of areas. I can sometimes convince myself that I am facilitating members of the public to travel to places further than the limited horizons of my cab. Often, there are servicemen on leave, perhaps merchant seamen reporting back to their ships, having spent a fortune in a short break. I must have driven world travellers, international businessmen, perhaps I am contributing in my small way to the world of industry and commerce, invention, and pleasure.

One minute I drive a lecturer and the next a student. The diversity of passengers and the never-ending variety of them and their destinations are a multitude, which when added together equate with bedlam. This equates with modern society in all its varieties. My cab helps glue the cosmos together....

People...

      ...traffic...

           ...time...

                  ...destinations.

Chapter 21
Pilot Trip to Israel

By 1969 we had only moved home 3 times, and next we thought to try somewhere warmer. Surely a cab driver could work anywhere in the world.

History told us, that of all the world's famous motorways, perhaps the oldest, is that which was trodden in biblical days by caravans, namely 'The Kings' Highway'. It was traversed by armies and camel trains between Egypt and Mesopotamia several millennia ago. We tried in the short space of two weeks, to find out how the cab trade was working in the middle part of that route, as we were considering settling in Israel. I specifically wanted to find out what it was like driving there, before we emigrated.

Landing in Israel well after nightfall, the first cab we used was from the EL AL bus terminal in Tel Aviv, situated in a greenish neighbourhood with no hotels visible. There was a lone taxi at the rank, possibly the driver only came out at night. I suspect he might well have been 'nicked' if he worked in the daylight hours, and the police spotted him. We needed a taxi both to cope with our luggage and to find us an hotel. We had not booked in advance. Internet was not available in those days. We were approached by the driver in knee length trousers, who both by his dress and age looked like an early settler. His cab must have arrived at the same time, for like a well ridden horse, it sagged in the centre. My wife and I carried our cases to the cab, in the company of the driver. He did not offer to help.

I told him how much we wanted to pay for the night – bed and breakfast. He replied that he knew of a good hotel. He inferred that the hotel I had half-heartedly suggested, was double the price. The length of material covering the *boards* upon which we sat did not disguise the dire state of the cab. But, not lulled into a false sense of comfort, we were sufficiently aware to note that the taxi meter was not running. I asked the reason. *Mumble mumble…*

163

Five minutes later I enquired again. This time it transpired that the cab was a wreck, and that it really was not worth fixing the meter!! We did not think we were overcharged, and we ended up in the only hotel of character we stayed in during our two weeks. It belonged to the same era as our driver and cab, the 1940s. But the hotel was as spotless and immaculate as any characterful hotel could have been. The next morning after breakfast, the hotel phoned for a radio taxi which came promptly, and we drove to a car hire firm. We did not keep that car as long as we had planned, for the price per kilometre was prohibitive, and was probably double the English equivalent. Driving was no problem for me. In Tel Aviv, the hooting of other cars *before the lights turned green,* seemed pointless. In Haifa, the respect for pedestrians on crossings was laudable. In Jerusalem, the pedestrian respect for traffic signals was astonishing.

In Jerusalem, we completed a touristic walk at the Rockefeller Museum in the eastern section. The museum was unfortunately closed for lunch, so I asked a nearby taxi what it would cost to Rechavia, one of Jerusalem's residential districts. We agreed on IL (Israeli Lira) 3. This was in pre-Shekel days. Again, no meter running. I asked for it to be started. It was. We arrived, and the meter showed more than the agreed price, but he accepted IL3.

The structure of the cab trade was so different to London's. The biggest change being, that there are two sorts of taxis in the country. The first is The *Jitney (Sherut)* taxi, which fills its seven seats, and drives from A to B at a fixed price per person. There were infrequent periods in London where cabs would use the same system. This type of taxi travels on any given route in competition with the bus lines. It is either within a city, or most successfully, inter-urban. The actual cost to the passenger is little more than the price of a bus ticket, but it is certainly faster, and usually offers more frequent departures than buses. *Sherut,* will pick up or set down *anywhere* on its fixed route. In addition, it is more comfortable.

The majority of regular taxis are called '*Specials*'. They belong to cooperative companies where the cab owner not only buys a company share, but also pays a rental. Special Cabs are restricted to those ranks which the individual company owns. These could be railway stations, large hotels, or important centres of town sites. Very few companies own centre of the road sites, hence Specials are sometimes stuck in alleyways and hidden from the potential random rider.

Frequently, passengers phone the Special Cab Company office and then the taxi is dispatched from the nearest rank. By the 1970s the cabs were radio controlled, thus linked directly to the office. Previously there was a telephone line to the rank.

The owners, who are closest to the table, would usually cream off the best of the 'out of town' jobs, especially as they were usually booked well in advance. The journeyman, me in the beginning, would get the hum drum daily jobs.

Peugeot taxi. Howard with daughters. The Red band identifies a Haifa Taxi. The Yellow sticker on rear window displays company and phone number. The number 9 on the plate means Haifa.

A couple of days later we set off from Jerusalem for Tel Aviv inside a *Sherut* taxi. The vehicle was the standard Checker Marathon, originally made in Kalamazoo, later in Chicago, between 1960-82. The doors and seating were perfectly designed for multiple passengers. It became the quintessential New York cab. Our Sherut fare was so low as to be unbelievable. I was impressed by our driver, who slowed to a walking pace on the motorway to scream at a villager mooning his way over the 3-lane highway. He exclaimed that the yokel was a danger to himself and to drivers. The boy sitting next to me in the 7- seater, was in turn impressed, when on a sharp corner near Latrun, we came upon a couple of his classmates, who he said, had never shown any sign of responsibility. Yet they had stopped their car on the *bend*, and were methodically spreading sand from a container, provided for that purpose. *They were covering an oil slick.*

While in Tel Aviv, we took a *Special* to either a Museum or shopping precinct whichever was the shortest journey. We were in ignorance, standing almost at the museum, so the driver with the international aplomb of cabbies, took us to the precinct, that being further away. On the return trip back to Jerusalem by Sherut, lulled by the warm wind from the open windows, and the music on the driver's radio, we soon fell asleep.

Next place to visit was Haifa where I had friends. We tried to catch a bus to the '*Sherut terminal*' but unable to fathom the public transport system, decided to walk until we saw a cab. We dragged ourselves up hill and down dale until at last we saw a cab. He stopped, but in his honesty, told us we were nearly there and drove off. Had we met the only moral driver?

The interurban price again, was low, astonishingly so. Seated in the Haifa *Sherut*, the last 5 remaining seats were soon filled. I made the error of opening a map to see which route the driver was taking. Spontaneously, the man next to me gave us an unwarranted running commentary on the sites and sights, on the way. Blah bah, blah bah.

This reminds me of the story of a security agent looking for Chaim Yankel in Shderot, he arrived in Palmach Street and asked where number 5 was. "Oh, are you looking for Chaim the secret service agent?". Everybody is a busybody about everybody's business. That is why no one has sex in the streets: a couple would be told how to do it.

The 161-kilometre journey, Jerusalem – Haifa was done in 3 hours. While in Haifa, we booked an Egged 3-day long bus tour of Galilee. The tour company Egged, brought us by cab from our hotel to the bus station at their expense. After that tour and another overnight in Haifa, we set off for the last leg of our holiday. At Haifa's bus station I had an enjoyable shouting discourse with the cab rank, full of drivers. We

arrived shlepping our cases, a task, at which by now we had become experts. We must have looked like a couple of oranges ripe for the plucking.
I had a camera draped around my neck and maps and pamphlets bulging from my pockets.

All the waiting taxi drivers' eyes bulged. "Tel Aviv?" they barked in unison. "NO" we replied without breaking step. Their faces fell. Then they rallied, abandoned the rank and kept pace with us, as we approached the entrance to the bus station building.

"Where then?"
"S'Dot Yam"

They looked at one another. Baffled. These were fields unknown. But after all I was the one with the camera and the maps.

"Where's that?"
"Caesarea".

Once more, they became animated. A price was quoted. Immediately lowered when I ignored them. Quickly doubled when I said I wanted it *all the way* and not just on the main road turn off (the *Sherut* does not veer from its designated route). When I did not accept their 'kind' offers, they screamed after me in revenge, that it was 8 kilometres off the highway. I laughed and told them "It is a lovely day – perfect for walking". After all, when is it 27 degrees Celsius and sunny in London?

We travelled by bus as planned, and hitched a lift for the 3 kilometres to the guest house we had booked. We spent a delightful three days beside the beach. On Sunday when we left, once on the main Road it took all of 30 seconds to trap a passing Sherut. There is little opportunity for a Sherut driver to overcharge, as the cash is passed from hand to hand till it reaches the driver; the same with change.

Tuesday, in Tel Aviv we found a free *'Special'*, but he had to finish his argument with his last passenger. He had unknowingly taken a 'There and back' to Holon (South Tel Aviv), and had stopped the clock on arrival at Holon. Back in Tel Aviv, he tried to charge what he thought was proper, the punter refused, and paid what he thought was adequate. I understood the situation only too well from my London experience.

Once we took another *'Special'*, whose driver picked up a friend who travelled with us. This is a socialist country, and we had to share the taxi with the driver's friend. Mid holiday our luggage on the roof of another Special was exposed to an autumnal shower. There was no extra charge for the rain. We had often paid double price for the luggage on the roof, before we discovered the real price. To round our trip off we had been woken up together with half of the neighbourhood, when our early morning pickup - Sherut arrived well before the booked time. He continued hooting until we arrived at his cab door at 05:00.

All this happened some 50 years ago. Times, habits, and even taxis have changed. Have the drivers?

Chapter 22
1970s Living in Haifa

By 1970 we had packed up, immigrated and relocated with our daughters to Israel. My world had changed. Having driven in London for twelve years I had now driven in Haifa Israel, for a further two. Haifa being Israel's third largest City, had then a population of 200,000 (today 300,000).

Workwise I had contacts with Haifa Achuza Cab Company, nevertheless I made enquiries as to what else I could do other than driving a taxi. One offer was to drive a *Sherut* taxi Tel Aviv-Eilat on the Red Sea. This would be a 350 km journey through the really hot Negev Desert. The roads then were not yet motorways. Somehow, I felt there were going to be nights away from home. I did not feel this was an attractive option. However, what I did do, was study to become a Certified National Tourist Guide. On completion of the course, I was qualified to guide in English, Dutch and Italian. Having a multi-strand income setup afforded me both financial flexibility, and alternative work options.

The British New Immigrant Society offered us an alternative, to buy a guest house and run it. The site was close to Natanya, but too far out from the city centre for it to be a viable proposition.

When we arrived as immigrants, we were housed in Upper Nazareth. So, when I started cabbing in Haifa, I had to commute there daily by bus. In those days in the 1970s, the country was poor, and the facilities matched. The buses had bars across the always open windows, in order to let in a cool breeze in, and at the same time, prevented passengers entering through them to avoid paying the fare. I travelled that route together with, not only passengers, but the livestock they carried, live chickens with their legs tied. The cheekiest was the goat which tried to stare me out, while it stood in the aisle facing me in my seat. Another day, nobody was pleased when a watermelon stored in the luggage rack rolled out and hit the floor with a noisy explosion.

It came as a surprise for me when the manager of the Haifa cab company to which I had an introduction, explained what he expected of me. There was a great deal of kindness in his behaviour to me as a new immigrant. He asked me to bus up to the top of the inhabited area of Haifa, which actually was within the parameters of the company's six ranks, and start to walk downhill until I reached the office. All he expected of me, was to learn the names of the streets I passed on my way down. For someone with practice of the London streets, this did not prove to be too hard a task, and within the shortest time I had learned enough to be let loose. All that was left was to do was the taxi driving test. I was in business.

Working there I was not called Howard, but 'English Two'. Another Englishman had preceded me as a journeyman and his name remained 'English', even though he had worked there for 20 years. His name was Shlomo Chinn from Liverpool. My main employment guiding tourists was seasonal, and never sufficed to cover all our expenses. Having completed my Guide course soon after arrival in Haifa I opted for it, as it was clearly the better paid of the two jobs. Taxi driving was admirable as a second string as it afforded some flexibility.

I worked for a number of bosses, owning a variety of cars, ranging from Peugeot to Mercedes, each with different change over times, and varying weekend hours. 7-seater Mercedes diesels are not uncommon, and are frequently requested if more than four punters are travelling. The 7-seater would then, obviously, take precedence in the rank queue and a four seater cab would have to wait for a normal booking.

It is not necessary to buy a 'station' (rank). Any *owner-driver* has the opportunity to operate both as a 'Sherut' stagecoach, or pick up off the street. If I had driven a 'Special' passenger to Tel Aviv, I could put on one of the Haifa bound Sherut ranks there, and work my way home earning on the return journey. Eventually, after dropping off most of the other passengers, a remaining rider may ask the Sherut driver to continue as a 'Special'. At which point, the driver will run his meter and the passenger will pay the extra for his personal journey.

If a passenger, who wants both the speed and privacy of a car as opposed to the bus and is in a hurry it is possible to pay for the empty places. Somewhere in my head is the thought that an arrangement can be made with the driver that if he picks up en route the passenger gets repaid. In any case both the driver and the passenger are happy to start the journey as soon as possible.

It was only in the 1960s that privately owned cars began to appear more frequently on the roads of Israel. There was at the foundation of the country, a feeling of austerity, and by the 1970s prosperity began to show itself. Even today (1970s) the ratio of cars to families is low. The country then, was not only poor but still starting up. From the early days of the state's existence, taxis had an entrenched position. They were fully established and were operating in Mandate days before Israel existed. The old Turkish law has become the accepted *status quo unless altered*. There is NO public transport in all of Israel on Saturdays – the day of rest, except for taxis. Haifa is the exception to this rule and buses run here as they always did in Mandatory days.

There was then (1970s) a six-day working week. Following biblical references, the Jewish day starts at sundown. Thus, from the start of the Sabbath i.e., Friday evening until Saturday night there is no official public transport. Haifa in conformity with the rest of the country, has no public buses or transportation during the Sabbath eve. However, thanks to the 1948 status quo, Haifa was an exception and is now lucky enough to legally allow the buses to run on the Sabbath. Residents utilised this facility to get to the beach and swim. Also, there were and are, buses from Haifa to Nazareth and Galilee during Saturday.

For the rest of the country during the Sabbath there is a skeleton service of Sherut taxis. Sherut taxis can thus exploit the absence of public transport. Specials remain too expensive for the money conscious, and there is no more than the normal demand for Specials. Institutions, Hotels, Hospitals, priority factories, all use taxis the same as usual on Saturdays.

In our company the good long journeys conveying staff from their various home addresses to work increases on Saturdays. There are factories which even on a weekday, use 20 cabs to get their workers in. These are in addition to the booked buses and transport trucks which usually move the majority of workers. The poor journeyman working on the Saturday has forms galore to fill in, documenting that the journey took place, so that the cab owner can produce the forms for the office to deal with, and ultimately be paid. These jobs provide few if any tips for the driver, and the driver receives a mere 30% of the price of the journey.

Some journeymen can work a 12-hour shift. Other paid drivers are those who have it as a second job, bank-clerks or perhaps soldiers on leave from the army. Lorry drivers, driving instructors, and students are amongst the many who occasionally sit behind the taxi steering wheel. Overall, in Israel one works longer hours than in London. Many have second jobs.

Driving a taxi in Israel is always a little unusual, and so I am content to wait for the unexpected to enliven the more mundane work. One Passover, while still driving a taxi in Haifa, I had the honour to deliver Matzah Shmura prior to the festival. What happened was that a senior Rabbi wanted to give this matzoh to important and seriously religious members of his congregation. This super sanctified unleavened bread, has from the moment of its reaping, been supervised by rabbinic authorities until its formation into Matza. So that no moisture will enter the grains of wheat before it is made into flour.

Matzo Shmura. The Matza is roughly 25cm diameter.

A Matzo Shmura is baked from wheat reaped from a supervised field and controlled from that moment until it reached its destination at the Seder table. For my participation in this good deed, I was given the last of the Matzos as a tip!!

There are no ploys that the London drivers operate which are not used here, and there are plenty of new ones to be learned. There is something exciting in being asked to drive to Nazareth, or an airport job which ends at Lud (today Ben Gurion Airport), or to take a Football Referee to a soccer match alongside the Sea of Galilee. These exotic destinations were for me compensation for the poor income.

Like most immigrants, I wanted to be accepted as a local as soon as possible, so to my chagrin, as soon as I spoke to someone who I had picked up and I had said the welcoming "Shalom" rather than "Hi", it immediately evoked the response "Oh you are English?". To this day, 50 years on, my English tongue enunciated Hebrew still chafes in my daughters' ears.

Our first home in Israel on the Carmel above the wadi. Our flat was in the second building from the top right.

In the beginning when we were living on the Carmel mountain in Haifa, I worked on Saturdays when the cab owner was down at the sea, swimming. It was a normal hot weather Saturday morning, when the dispatcher told me to pick up a football referee and take him to and from a match that he was refereeing that afternoon. I still do not know whether I was given the job because of my newness, and was thus unaware of potential trouble, or because I was new and deserved a good job. I was pleased to take the job – a trip into the Galilee and a chance to read a book and earn money, all at once. As usual, taxis on long jobs earn by time as well as distance. We arrived in good time and the ref. changed into his working togs and left his usual clothes in the cab. I settled down stretched out in the back seat, and heard the occasional roars of excitement that accompany any crowd event. I brought my nosh with me into the back seat, the heat was not bad, as we were high in the hills. The book was good the nosh tasty.

Shfaram, an Arab team were playing a Tel Aviv team at home, and the excitement began to build as the game progressed. I guessed correctly there would be some nationalism attached to the match, but that was scarcely an issue for me. After a particularly long shout, I heard a few pops, and thought someone has burst a balloon or two, until slowly the quantity of pops entered my awareness and I realised these were *pistol shots. I sat up in my seat and swivelled my* attention to the pitch, and there I could just see the local police with firearms in their hands facing irate spectators.

The game was nearing its end, and while I was evaluating this event, the referee accompanied by a few cops was rushed into the cab, and I was told to follow the police car that had just pulled up in front of me. We left the ground with a second police car behind us and drove up the hill to their station. It took a couple of hours wait before they considered tempers had calmed, and it was safe to escort my cab out of their jurisdiction. Driving without an escort, we were able to relax on the remainder of the homeward bound journey back to Haifa.

I had not been working with Carmel Ahuza Taxi Company Ltd. long, before the manager to encourage, not just a butter boy, but a new immigrant, gave me a job to the then Lydda/Lod airport: the airport later became renamed after Ben Gurion the first Prime Minister. The manager and dispatcher had both asked, would I be able to find my way there, some 100 kilometres away. Big -headed me, was well aware that there were adequate road signs even though it was dark. The pickup was at night, and the couple which I was to transfer were ready and waiting when I arrived. Being a healthy 40-year-old, I jumped out, and with two weightlifters jerks put the largest and heaviest bag onto the roof. The weight of the suitcase was such that *I knew nothing would dislodge it from the roof rack.*

Off we set down the mountain onto the coast road, and I thought "what can go wrong", me reaching the legal speed limit of 100 kph. About 20 kilometres down the seaside highway in the darkness, the only light being the headlights of travelling vehicles, we suddenly heard a strange scraping on the roof and then a sort of thump and then silence. All three of us knew what had happened. I slowed the cab, pulled over and parked. The husband and I started to walk back to where we had just been. Surreptitiously, I stole glances into the motorway praying the case had not landed there. My prayers were answered, for the case began to be illuminated by oncoming headlights, and we both rushed to pick it up off the roadside verge. Returning to the cab, I hastened to bind the case securely to the rack not giving the wind any more chances to wreak havoc with the valise. For whatever reason, the couple were more stoic about the event than I, and having followed what road signs there were, we arrived at BG in good time and parted company as friends.

Many moons later, I was again given a job to Ben Gurion. I was delighted for it meant both good money and a chance to leave the city area. This time it was in the early morning, and after being given a "Hurry up, will you?" from the dispatcher, for the first and only time in my life, I managed to water-plane, when approaching the roundabout on the main road about one kilometre from the rank. It had been raining and I had accelerated, so as not to be too late at the pickup point.

As I approached the flower decorated roundabout, I slowed down to drive around it. The steering did not respond for I was driving on a slim sheet of water, and even though the front road wheels responded and turned, the forward momentum continued, the taxi going dead ahead.

The steering had no effect as the wheels were not on the road but on the sheet of rainwater which covered the entire approach. No matter how I turned the steering wheel, the forward motion had its say. The brakes were futile in that situation. Sadly, I mounted the roundabout, and the marks I caused remained there for many a month. The grass surround and the broken stone wall were there for all to see. It taught me a lesson. The damage to the car was not bad. Naturally the job was given to the next cab on the rank.

Afterwards, I had to decide whether to pay up for any damage I had caused to the Mercedes, and decided it was 100% my fault and paid for the smallish repair. Even after that experience and quickly admitted fault, I don't believe I had any problems finding another owner who would let me drive his cab. I now respect roads with a thick coating of water.

Chapter 23
Yerushalayim

Having moved once again. 1984, sees me taxi driving in the capital city of Israel, Jerusalem. Only a cab driver constantly transiting the streets can feel the mood of the city as he floats slowly through different areas looking for work, watching and meeting a variety of citizens from most walks of life. The variations are frequent, simultaneously challenging, and often stimulating. Different components of the mixed city vary from day to day, place to place, and even by times of day.

As I drive, I note Arab, Jew, ultra-orthodox, and secular. The changes are both in pedestrians and neighbourhoods, even football stadia. There are Arab bus stations with passengers to the West Bank and beyond, travelling on buses run by Arab companies. Passengers are swathed in traditional garb against the hot sun. Now I see a Jewish bus station where Egged has a near monopoly of the Jewish Bus lines. Each sight is so close to the next that the transformation has to be quickly registered. There are places in Jerusalem where you can be stoned (literally!), for driving on the Sabbath (Saturday). Three holy days a week is a challenge. Fridays for Muslims, Saturdays for Jews and Sundays for Christians.

In the same manner that I became acquainted with the moods of London, I was becoming aware of my new hometown as I familiarised myself with the roads.

I have guided tourists in Israel for 14 years. Churches, Hotels, Restaurants, and excavations are all my bread and butter, and now in Jerusalem, the roads and boulevards are a new source of income, coupled with the frisson of an expansive variety of citizens. I am well aware of the nearest police station, and the first aid centre for each of the sites, not to mention the best coffee shops for my Dutch pilgrims. As a tour guide, I am competent to sit under the copy of The Last Supper painting, housed in Dormition Abbey, and can discuss the symbolism in the more than twenty hands and finger gestures of the disciples. I am slowly beginning to penetrate the idiosyncrasies of this living city. Daily, my experiences are building my understanding of behaviour and events in this Mediterranean metropolis.

It takes experience and understanding to comprehend who is flowing into and out of that 'Tower of Babel' – the Jerusalem Bus Station. Visitors, pilgrims, businesspeople and simple plain residents returning home. The cab ranks, legal and illegal, cater quickly and efficiently with the swarms bursting out of the front doors of the Central Bus Station. Every day Police and soldiers stand by, monitoring those entering and leaving.

Driving further down the Jaffa Road towards the Old City, the Machane Yehuda fruit and vegetable market, with its wide variety of fresh and cooked foods, is a second potpourri of characters. There are the poor who are on the lookout both for bargain prices of commodities nearing the end their shelf life, plus all the fruit and vegetables that are daily discarded as over ripe. There are the wealthy who come to scoop up a week's shopping at low prices. A cab driver stops, collects a fare, moves on. Is he driving a vendor who has made a small fortune? The driver chatting with his passenger covertly assesses who the rider is.

Cab driving anywhere in the world offers the attraction of never knowing what the next job will bring. Jerusalem is comparatively small and poor. Few people own cars, so more than usual out of town jobs turn up. Sometimes the rides are remunerative other times they will kill a day's work. But for me they all add to my ever-growing knowledge of the country.

Wham! The three lads were in the cab before I could say Jack Cohen. Once sprawled all over the seats, they told me their destination. I was not pleased: Neve Yaakov- a northern suburb. But I doubted I could get them to leave the cab peacefully. I settled for the lesser of the two evils and drove off listening to their patter. Neve Yaakov is established in an all-Arab environment. It is one of a ring of new towns built since 1967, to surround Jerusalem as part of a strategic and demographic plan for the Capital City and the West Bank. Its umbilical road connection to Jerusalem is vital for both work and pleasure. There is little in this suburb other than housing (1980s). Taxi rides to Neve Yaakov are a waste of time, for few people ride back to town by cab. Time and fuel are forfeited on the cab's return to work.

They spoke Hebrew, but effortlessly changed to Russian and back again. Obviously all three were immigrants from Russia. Further conversation revealed that at least two of the three were cooks. This not being London, the driver is privy to all the conversations that take place while he is driving. There is no glass partition behind his back. One of the lads worked at a shiny new hotel, and another at an older establishment. At the new hotel the lad felt he was being exploited, and planned to quit. Further dialogue revealed that the cook at the larger older hotel was intending to continue his career in the US.

Blanking out the chatter, I mused what this guy's parents thought about this plan. Somehow, the family had carved out a home here in Israel, certainly no easy transition for them, from Russia to Israel. Yet now this son and daughter in law were leaving. Was it for a better income, was it to avoid military service? Was it for an easier life? Perhaps it was merely to fulfil the desire for adventure. I deposited them one by one, at their destinations, and chatted up the last one to supplement my picture of the trio.

Starting the journey back, to my surprise I was hailed by a solid looking Slav woman and her daughter who hailed me from the wrong corner of the road, leading away from Jerusalem. I edged towards them not quite making the turn, leaving my driving options open. They asked for Moshav Adam.

I had never heard of it. Just North of here they said, only 6 kilometres away via the Arab towns of A Ramah and Jaba. I decided that I was so far North of Jerusalem another 6 kilometres would make no difference. Off we set. I was truly curious. The woman was built like a bulldozer possibly of peasant stock, and her daughter a mere slip of a girl around 7 or 8 years old. They had been shopping for schoolbooks for the new school year. Textbooks were bought by parents, and each year they changed hands when the new school year started. They told me that the lass was bused daily to her school, in the North Jerusalem suburb of French Hill.

There is always a feeling of anticipation at the start of the new school year, and I could sense it in the youngster too. Who would be her class teacher? Will it be better than last year? Which clubs will she join? Will

179

the birthday parties that are usually attended by most of the class include her?

At A Rama we turned off the main road; the Arab village is mentioned twice in the bible, in both Joshua and Samuel. In fact, Rama means a high place in English, and it is mentioned many times in the old and new testaments. Driving through it, I had a slight apprehension, this was not my milieu. My two female passengers were not bothered. Maybe they were used to driving through there - I did not ask. Later that day listening to the news broadcast, I learned that a house in A Rama had been sealed off by the Army. It was the home of a terrorist discovered only this week. He had recently been operating in the West Bank. This village highlighted the race of development on the lands of the West Bank, during the past decade.

Whoever has property on the land establishes title to the land. An approximate understanding, perhaps relating to a law during the Ottoman period, that continues to this day. So there has been an attitude of 'build now – think later'. Any Arab getting permission from the Israeli authorities to build is entitled to a substantial grant from King Hussein's Government in Jordan. Incidentally, it was King Hussein who donated the gold leaf for the roof of the *Dome of the Rock on the Temple Mount*. He financed his philanthropy by selling a London home to pay for it.

Thus, superstructure goes up. Sometimes the houses are absurdly superb villas, otherwise they are within the normal span of rural development. What is frequently lacking is a path to them, and Water, Electricity and Sewage! But the property is established, and with it the right of possession of the land. The point is made. Either Jewish Settlers or Arab Landowners. With the birth of a Jewish Settlement the amenities are brought in. This is frequently expensive and the financial value of the entire exercise is debatable.

A Rama is developing fast not just to prove this point, but because there is potential for new shops with apartments above. The shop signs I saw were in Arabic, but I noticed frequent English signs too. Which suggests perhaps, non-Arabic-reading shoppers.

Before we came to Jaba, also mentioned in the bible as Gibeah, my riders told me to use the 'new road' which bypassed Jaba. Security wise, I was unhappy to drive in the new man-made canyon thrust through the tops of the hills. Driver-wise I was unhappy to drive over two and a half kilometres of rocky dusty substructure. The only plus is that like many of our new roads it was straight and almost without inclines. Arriving at Moshav Adam I was not surprised I had never heard of it. Some 20 Mobile homes were perched on the terrain. This was where the pair had lived for the past year or so. It was guarded by a single soldier sitting in a chair in the middle of the caravans. No trees, not even newly planted midget saplings were to be seen. Perhaps this was not precisely to be their final settlement site. More astoundingly, I could not identify a single section of perimeter fence. A daylight guard, WOW! My passengers deserved all of my respect.

Many settlements have night time guards but a daylight one is not an auspicious sign. Perhaps under its second reincarnation name, 'Givat Benjamin' it needs to be less guarded. 2022 shows it now has some 5,000 settlers. I drove back to Jerusalem sobered by the thought that pioneering in Israel is not dead. I had not then thought the matter through and realised that this kind of establishment would become a bone of major contention between Israel and the remainder of the world. I could not but help admire the courage and tenacity of the settlers, yet simultaneously, I harboured serious doubts of the economic and strategic wisdom of this type of site.

Thinking in this way, I had to ignore the demographic strategic significance of Israelis positioned there in the Judean Hills. I have not even mentioned the other West Bank settlements. The settlement of Moshav Adam, was then, and is now the epitome of contention. Right or wrong?

Arriving back in Jerusalem in search of a fare, I went down into Sanz and then Belz, a pair of Chassidic religious districts. Since there is little money in these districts, car ownership is negligible. I passed a religious couple with a baby. Was that a signal? Out of the corner of my eye I had caught the last phase of an arm movement, a black coated sleeve returning downwards. I stopped the car 100 meters on and looked in the rear view mirror. This time I caught the upwards movement as well. The man was trying to hail me, with a flagging arm movement.

I let the car roll backwards down the slope towards them. They wanted to go to the Wailing (Western) Wall, but did not want to pay the three and a half shekels I suggested. "Could you do it for 3 shekels?" I gave a firm "No", and off we set. I explained that the Jaffa Gate was closed today because of road works in the Jewish Quarter of the Old City of Jerusalem, and that I would leave them at the Dung Gate which was as close as I could drive to The Wall.

They told me to expect crowds. "Why?" I asked. They told me that a new children's' Torah scroll had been completed. The Pentateuch scroll had been subscribed letter by letter. Each letter donated by another child. The conversation revealed that the cost of the parchment, scribe and time was (and is) immense. This particular scroll had been created by the 'Chabad' Chassidic court. Sitting in a traffic hold-up, we tried to discover how many letters there were in a scroll but somehow became involved in the vowels which are not actually letters. I became confused and dropped the subject.

I have since learned and sometimes practice, the religious injunction of mentioning religious matters during every conversation, sometimes hearing fresh understandings of the law. Otherwise, conversation is religiously totally pointless.

Here as in London promoting conversation is a driver's stock in trade; indeed, it makes the time fly. There are an infinite number of gambits for this, but Jerusalem is the only place where I have been able to discuss the origin of the street names and to receive a learned set of replies. "This street is named after the author who lived here in the forties" "This street is named after a book written by..." "No, someone else wrote that book..." "It's named after a type of Rifle", "That street is named after 43 heroes who died defending this area of Jerusalem in the War of Independence, the street incidentally has 43 buildings".

Explanation. Contradiction, explanation. The simplest solution is to read the street signs at the ends of each road. Municipalities throughout the country add thumbnail biographies to the street names. Whether the name is of a musician or of a country, there is often a story attached. In fact, one of the local journalists has printed a collection, of the origins of the street names. All street signs are in Hebrew, Arabic, and English.

I have even deliberately mistranslated the name of the street where I lived, Partridge Street, and renamed it 'The Partridge Family', of television fame.

In Jerusalem my local bus line drives through the identical mish mash of districts which what happens to me in a day's driving. With the bus it is done in half an hour. It mixes and serves a cocktail of passengers all in one glass, or if you wish, one bus. At my end of my route 7, there is a study centre based in the Kibbutz Ramat Rachel. The first passengers on this line are not only kibbutz members, guests and students, but also come from the Arab Village of Tsur Bahar.

As the bus leaves the kibbutz terminus, the passengers are already a mixture. Tourists, students, and plain bourgeois home dwellers. First destination: the centre of town, where immediately the seats are filling with modern and very religious Jews. By the far end of the route there will not be one woman sitting next to a man who is not related to her. It is simply not possible for a religious man to sit next to any female to whom he is not married. Once a kind passenger solved this problem for me by getting up and moving further back inside the bus, so that I could take his place. My wife was now adjacent to me the other side of the central aisle, but in the 'women's section'.

On another occasion, before we left Tel Aviv's Bus Station Sherut rank, we were asked in a friendly manner for me to yield the favoured seat where I was already sitting next to the driver, so that a religious man would not have the horror of sitting next to a woman. I refused. This incident has reminded me that a religious man will probably lose his mind if he walks between two women. Which in any case, is nearly as bad as a truly religious adherent who listens to a female singer. He might just…

There is a divide in Jerusalem's Arabs and Jews. Arabs live in the East and Jews in the West, but I must immediately contradict this: there are pockets of both groups in the opposite sections and even more so on the outskirts. I can frequently suss out whether a punter is a Jew or not, but cannot easily see the difference from Sephardi and Ashkenazi Jews, except for their speech. I have had many journeys when a party of Iraqi, Moroccan or Yemeni Jews do not speak a word of Ivrit (modern Hebrew) during the entire journey. I have heard a class of English speech which is fast disappearing, used by those who grew up in British Mandate Palestine, it can be heard in a hoarse timbre echoing the tone of the "Tommies" stationed in Palestine during the British Mandate.

Nevi'im street (the street of the prophets), Jerusalem is part of a religious neighbourhood. Working there night after night, I feel that I am living in the books of Shalom Aleichem, written in eastern Europe, a century past. The Shtetl village life becomes alive to me. The ambience draws me back night after night.

Many riders though competent in Hebrew (Ivrit), speak the argot tongue Yiddish which they use daily, either to confuse me, be rude, or because they believe that Ivrit is truly exclusively the 'Holy Tongue' of prayer. Any use of modern Hebrew for the mundane, is a desecration of the Holy Tongue.

Each Rabbi has his opinion on this matter. Members of each individual rabbi's congregation follow his lead. Most of the days' time is dedicated to study of the law, the Talmud, but by eventide the pace has slackened. Their residential areas now burst with life. The streets begin to fill.

Women too, relax in the cooler air. They appear, each wearing stockings, and headgear which hides their hair. The men must not be attracted to them. No matter how hot a day, the fully bearded men appear clad in their traditional black garments. The more modern men trim their beards. The majority sport tightly curled sidelocks. Some sideburns descend and are then curled back behind the ears. The beard colour varies with the owner, the angle at which the beard projects from the chin is highly individual.

Driving the cab one bus stop further into the centre of town, and hey presto, I see women on the sidewalk tottering on high heels displaying bare backs and smoking as they walk. The mystic aura has vanished. The charisma of Jerusalem is the experience of these juxtapositions, night after night, day after day. Yes, you can see it all in 24 hours, but it is the subtle differences which appear as the months pass: each is a particular nuance which creates the intriguing variety of sights. The different neighbourhoods, house adherents to different rabbis, each with minor variations of the single religion of Judaism, hence the variation in clothing. Socks and hats often indicating the original East European villages and hamlets from where they originated.

"Yossi! Whip us up to Anata! We will only be there a minute and then we will be coming back". With nearly three decades of cabbing behind me I know here is potential trouble. The lads are out to buy drugs. Maybe they will not pay me, or maybe do a 'runner'. All's well.

Five minutes later an eight-year-old girl is put into the cab. American accents. I talk to the child in English. She replies. Then all I have to do is say "Yes", as she rattles on. The girl explains she had been called to help her mother in a downtown restaurant. Dad has been called up for the Army Reserves and is out somewhere sleeping on the stones. I empathise with the dad's description of how he removes an offending stone from under him, only to find that there are now two. His eloquent daughter continues with his tale. I empathise with him again, in his daughter's tale of struggle with the local authorities. The licensing authority is trying to prise fees from him for previous years when he was not the owner of the restaurant. A bureaucratic mistake, but when will it end? The sophisticated youngster's chatter slows as we approach her home. "I do hope you will not cheat me with the change – the man in the grocery store does!". It's time to return the cab to its owner. The streets are beginning to empty, and my eyelids are becoming heavy.

Chapter 24
Tiberias

March 2000 provided me with a memory which remains clear in my mind to this day. It was the week that Pope John Paul II visited the Holy Land. He stopped at the Jewish Western Wall in Jerusalem where he in traditional manner left a note in the wall. The five-day visit starting at Ben Gurion airport where he was greeted by the then President, Ezer Weizman. His visit included Bethlehem and Nazareth. Next, John Paul, the first Pope in recent history to visit Israel, travelled to the Sea of Galilee, en route visiting Korazin on the Mount of Beatitudes. There are archaeological remains of a village, probably about the size of *biblical* Korazin. The settlement contained perhaps a thousand residents in the time of Jesus.

Jesus' Galilean ministry was centred round Capernaum. The stone walls visible today are from a later period around the third or fourth Century. The village has archaeological remains predating Jesus's Ministry. Tradition names Kfar Nahum as the home of St. Peter.

I was touring, but had been given the Sunday off so that the group could have time to themselves on the Christian Sabbath. We were in Tiberias, situated on the bank of the inland Sea, and I was sipping coffee at a restaurant table. The flow of tourists passing was much more than usual, frequently being 50 strong groups of pilgrims. They descended from their tour buses and were strolling eagerly, imbibing the atmosphere of the promenade of the landlocked Sea of Galilee.

Some tourists would have already been to Capernaum and Korazin. Others would go later in the day. Some would join a tour boat and see where the fishermen who became disciples, had cast their nets. The St. Mark's gospel reports how Jesus stilled the storm there. There was a joie de vivre in the air created by exuberant youngsters swarming past, certain of their futures. They were happy, full of their beliefs, their youth and destinies. They sang and danced as they bustled their way along the sea's shore.

I noted tourists and pilgrims from the world over. Tiberias is a regular tourist attraction, but this was a special week. Notable, were the flags of European countries particularly, and from South America and Poland, the Pope's homeland. Luggage and outfits frequently boasted national flags.

The super joy and exuberance of the event that day, wafted by happily in the hot summer breeze. The limestone walls of the old buildings visible from where I sat, gleamed with pride at this visit by a Pope. I too, was and am, taken by my fortune at being present to this Galilean one-time episode, marking happenings from two thousand years ago.

In between the tourists, came two priests wearing blue peaked caps to ward off the spring sunshine. Now, eight American women chattering, and then a bunch of Dutch. Next came a bunch of pilgrims who had their name tags blazoned on their rucksacks, and I realised with a smile, that anyone overtaking them would know their names and be able to greet them without the embarrassment of being caught staring. Then I saw someone else with the same fashion, and I knew that if the Pope had remained longer, it would have been a la mode all over the country.

A quick glance skyward revealed three levels of birds imitating the peregrinations of the land bound pilgrims. Directly above the man-made harbour, where the water was warmer and where the fishing boats were moored, was the hover location for the fishing birds with long downwards pointed beaks, searching for the stationary prey of fishes luxuriating in the warmth of the shallow seaside. The swallows made the most noise with their cheery chirruping, as they made their mercurial dashes to their nests in and on the sunroofs of the fish restaurants, nimbly settling down in the comfort of their favourite haunts. Way above, floating in the blue sky were birds which scavenge anything edible.

Sitting there glancing at the daily newspaper the Jerusalem Post, my concentration was broken by the cadences of several hand drums. Soon the beating was joined by a guitar. Next, several young people began to join the rhythm in song. Then about a dozen young girls formed themselves into a circle dancing to the beat. The circle broke and rejoined, as individuals moved to the centre and then out again, while their hands and arms gracefully echoed the tempo.

My waiter constantly attempted to lure people into his restaurant, but they were all too busy talking and looking. I knew that they would be back later in the day when they were tired and hungry. Most on a tour would have had their meals provided by the hotels in which they were staying. I moved my gaze to my right, over the cobalt sea to observe the heights of the Golan Mountains on the far side of the water.

There was at that moment, a group posing themselves in a photo which decades later would turn into a 'Where is he/she now' photo. Meanwhile further away, a group was boarding a launch with illuminated masts and rigging, the light from the bulbs outlining every feature of the vessel. Eventide had crept up.

The hubbub of the masses ebbed and flowed, as did the size of each group. Occasionally, I stopped my reading to try and trace the source of a particularly melodious song, and when I finally located the sound, it came from the sea where a group had begun a brief trip. Sometimes the national flag of those on board the motor launch, fluttered on their boats' mast. Their exuberance in no way diminished, their music merrily continued. The tune from one boat took me back to two days previously, when I had heard the "Shema Yisroel" ("Hear O Israel") from Deut.6 and Mark 12.29 being sung in the Church of All Nations in Gethsemane in Jerusalem. It again sung in Hebrew this time to the beat of Ravel's Bolero. Perhaps it was the same group. The constantly rising Bolero beat is with me still.

The most rousing song happened that afternoon, when a really large group passing by sung 'Land of Milk and Honey' in Hebrew. The Israeli guide leading them was definitely not holding up a religious icon, as they powered their way through the crowds. It was simply a sheet of A4 paper, the Hebrew words boldly printed in English letters. The people that wanted to sing walked closely behind him so that they could both read the text and sing together as they progressed. They had a Brazilian Flag, and halfway through the group, there was another person holding a second copy. But those at the rear of the group were not as enthusiastic as the leaders. Another crowd walking in the opposite direction heard them coming and enthusiastically catching the syncopation, clapped a counter beat. It was a magnificent moment. Eventually, the Tiberias sun did its disappearing act above the upper city, then a cacophony of recorded music drifted over to me. Peering towards its source, I saw a record salesman from a shop launching Spanish style music, and his bystanders responded with boisterous dance steps and gestures. Beneath me at sea level one after the other, four fishermen arrived preparing their boats for the night's work; ill shaven and warmly dressed for the night air, they began to prepare the lights for the nets and the large light attached to the boat which would attract the fish. There was a little friendly banter between them, and off they set into the gathering dusk. As they left the tiny harbour, 8 canoes that I had seen earlier in the afternoon arrived, the paddlers looking well contented as they raced one another into the mooring area. Two were not as swift as the others. The brave sight they had made as they left their moorings a couple of hours ago, eight canoes in single file, was not repeated.

Sunday, being the day off for the local Christian community, the usual routine of boys out in their Sunday best looking for the local talent, was not working. There were far too many tourists ruining the normal easy contact. The normal quips and trysts did not occur. Nothing was left for me now but to return to the hotel and watch on television, the Pope boarding his plane prior to his departure to Rome, while the house lights on the Golan Heights lit up almost in sequence, and twinkled their way across the Kinneret Sea of Galilee.

End Piece

Egypt and Israel signed a peace treaty in 1979. The return of the Sinai peninsula to Egypt by Israel, was taking place section after section. The fifth such return of land conquered in the Six Day War of 1967 was soon to occur.

One night, I must have had a late-night job to Tel Aviv, and stayed over with friends. Next morning, I went down the stairs from the third floor to find shards of glass in lieu of my cab. Dismayed, I looked here and there thinking I had forgotten where I had parked it, but no I had not forgotten! In reality the broken glass was all that was left of my investment. Distraught, dismayed and transport less, I now needed immediately to inform my co-driver partner that our 7 - passenger seat Mercedes taxi, was gone.

The details became clearer when it was simplified for me. Jewish thieves would steal the most expensive vehicles available. Usually, the cars would need be broken up and the parts sold individually – now the cars could be sold whole. The vehicles would be hidden under the sand in a section of land that was soon to be handed over to Egypt.

A local taxi took me to Jaffa, the nearest Police Station, where I was treated as I always seem to be if I enter a police Station, as a suspicious person. Eventually, I proved my bona fides. Explanations and murmurs and were made, informing me of many such thefts in the area. Within a short period of talking with other drivers and paying more attention to the press, I realized that I was caught up in international politics.

A couple of years earlier, wing mirrors and windscreen wipers could disappear whenever and wherever I parked my Volkswagen minibus. Driving through the streets of Tel Aviv, they or their equivalent parts were offered for sale at traffic lights. Great fun – but this time it was serious. My partner and I debated every possibility, and when speaking to our office, *Carmel Ahuza*, where we ranked, we found to our delight that we could breathe a sigh of relief, for the drivers' committee had kept up with the times. They had paid for the vehicle insurance to cover the *hyperinflation*, which in those weeks, increased daily at 12:00. That is another story, but it meant that when and if we were paid out, we would get the up to the minute value. Phew.

Thinking we were clever we decided to descend into the Gaza Strip, always notorious for terrorists. Together, we would search in all the garages we could find to look for our vehicle before it was broken up. Naively unaware of the sophisticated theft mechanism which was in place. We were perhaps putting ourselves in danger. Arriving there and beginning our search sooner rather than later, we realised this was an exercise in futility, and we promptly returned safely to Israel proper. Nothing more we could do.

Within a week the newspapers were running a story which we read avidly. It concerned Israel's withdrawal from the last 7,000 acres of Sinai. Urban Arabs, now the recipients of high spec stolen cars were selling them on to Bedouin. The vehicles were driven deep into Sinai, wrapped carefully, so the sand would not penetrate into or onto the car's surface, and then buried. The car would remain concealed and warm, until one day in the near future, the border would change – the vehicle would now be in Egypt, with no more bother from Israeli Police. No border to cross. It might in some circles, even be considered war booty. A trophy much admired.

The article went on to relate how a member of Israel's parliament – the Knesset, Samuel Flatto Sharon, a multi-millionaire, had lost his super de lux Mercedes Benz. Out of sheer frustration, he had paid for helicopter flights over the soon to be Egypt areas, in search for his and other stolen cars. The flights would look for disturbed mounds of freshly uncovered sand. Over a 15-year period, Israeli Police working this area had retrieved about 400 vehicles including Peugeots and Volvos. They were also buried there under the sand. At the time of our taxi being stolen roughly a quarter of all buried vehicles had been unearthed by Israeli search teams.

Searchers investigating, could drive right by a vehicle and not notice it, as they passed. The canvas or sacking wrapping not only kept out the sand but disguised the shape. Other aerial surveys were done to aid the police in their search. This was the fifth and last withdrawal, and the desert with its buried vehicles would soon be in Egypt. There to be reinvented with Egyptian number plates, and could be driven around Egypt with little query. Much trouble was taken to make the cars look local, and wind shield stickers in Egyptian helped the disguise.

Ultimately, we received the insurance money, and were in a position to replace the lost Mercedes. We decided not to, and I shifted my half of the money to the UK, and it became a prelude for my driving a taxi in London once again.

It was a Passover night some years later, when we were sitting around the table in Jerusalem eating Matzos, when I had a phone call from an excited policeman. He told me that my taxi had been found entering the Ben Gurion airport. I was thrilled and thanked the officer for his news. I had barely sat down when I realised that an injustice had been done. I phoned back and explained that my taxi plate *number* had been mine all along, and it was being leased out, as is the normal custom. My next rent began on the morning after the phone call, it would be mounted on a different taxi.

What had happened was that the detained driver had been using his old plates till the morrow, and then on the due date he would take off the old plate and expose mine underneath. This system is still used by attaching the old plate with wire over the new one about to be used. My new renter was released when I explained that the engine and chassis numbers would not match those of the stolen vehicle. Then we continued with the Passover (Pesach) Seder.

Chapter 25
The Third String

Over the years, in Jerusalem, it became clearer that I needed a third string to my bow. Occasional cabbing was not viable in Jerusalem. In Haifa, I had a father figure in the office, who would help me find a cab if I needed to do some work as a journeyman. In Jerusalem a minor anarchy reigned. There were the two usual types of cabs Special and Sherut. But, there was a massive fleet of taxis driven by the East Jerusalem drivers, who frequently would agree a price and not run the meter. Prices were then undercut. Unless one used the telephone to book a cab, the punter could not be sure of the driver, price, or route. This was not a milieu in which I wished to compete.

Even though I could still lease out my number plates, and with my guiding, mainly pilgrims, I could make ends meet. My wife worked in a shop. In 1981, off I set for London, and for a visit to the PCO The last time I had been there was 1970 prior to moving to Israel. Then, in a fit of self-abnegation, I had returned my Bill. I rationalised that by holding it while I was away, I would be depriving a Knowledge Boy of a job. Here I was again in 1981, this time lodging with my sister Valerie in Wembley, and redoing the Knowledge.

I was given guidance by a good friend from Chiswick, Martin Kingsley who was involved with driving instruction at the LTDA. I remember one day driving in a cab under his instruction, when I hesitated before entering a narrow entrance. I knew I could do it, but I did not want to appear too much of a bighead. I asked what to do, and he said, "If you can get through it. Do it". Within 6 months I saw my Bill back in my pocket. Mucking in with other Knowledge Boys was not quite the thing for me, for bubbling in my head were places and streets from a decades ago. One Ways altered, right turns forbidden, shops come and gone. Old blocks of flats disappeared, replaced with new ones with new names, major shops gone and others equally important in their place.

I now had my third string, and started to commute to London with my wife every winter. We rented flats in various places and it fell into a rhythm, summer Israel, London winter. Reaching retirement age, we decided to return to the UK completely. And I drove a cab for a couple of months each year. I made the most of the cab rental costs, by working 28 days straight off. This sum was enough to bolster our savings for the year. Martin from the LTDA used to drive only on Sundays, and this gave him enough cash to last the week.

Today in 2022 I am amputee. When travelling locally, I raise the phone and ask for a cab, in order to ride as a passenger. Visiting London theatres, we travel by underground to Chancery Lane Station. I work my way out of the station and stand on the South side of Holborn, hail a cab and let the driver cope with the turmoil on High Holborn.

My left leg is amputated above the knee, but I am allowed to drive to this day. However, the PCO demanded a doctor's opinion on my general health. My GP, in the process of retiring himself, did not want to be bothered. He wanted no responsibility for my possible future health problems apropos of driving a taxi. I decided that to pay for a full physical examination would cost more than I could earn when added to the cost of cab rental, so I decided to lodge my Bill. This was the moment for which the Carriage Office had been waiting. They sent me the standard 'Thank You' for years of work. This book is my testament.

Acknowledgements

This book has travelled twice across Europe, in the form of typewritten pages, and finally, has arrived in print, thanks to my wife who preserved the typescript, and then suggested I finally publish it. Her methodical fastidiousness kept me from printing gibberish.

I had the skilled aid of Tony Matthews to convert the book into digital form, and it was a family effort that pushed the final book into shape.

I must admit, some of the comments seem 'unwoke', but this was mostly written in 1962, and times they are a changing.

I must not forget Manny my friend, and his son who steered me forwards.

So, thanks to one and all, and I hope that YOU enjoyed all you read.

Printed in Great Britain
by Amazon